INDIAN INNOVATORS

20 BRILLIANT THINKERS
WHO ARE CHANGING INDIA

I0041152

AKSHAT AGRAWAL

JAICO PUBLISHING HOUSE

Ahmedabad Bangalore Bhopal Bhubaneswar Chennai
Delhi Hyderabad Kolkata Lucknow Mumbai

Published by Jaico Publishing House
A-2 Jash Chambers, 7-A Sir Phirozshah Mehta Road
Fort, Mumbai - 400 001
jaicopub@jaicobooks.com
www.jaicobooks.com

INDIAN INNOVATORS
ISBN 978-81-8495-659-7

First Jaico Impression: 2015
Tenth Jaico Impression: 2018

Page design and layouts: Fidus Design

Dedicated to my teacher, Shri Vineet Swarankar,
without whom I could not have achieved what I did...

Gurur Brahmaa Gurur Vishnu
Gurur Devo Maheshwarah
Guru Saakshaata Parabrahma
Tasmai Shri Guruve Namah

Acknowledgements

This book would not have been possible without the cooperation of all those who have been featured herein. Each one of them showed great support and encouragement for the idea and generously gave their time for the interviews, despite busy schedules. I thank them from the bottom of my heart for honestly sharing their stories with me.

I especially thank Mrinmayee Bhushan for penning a section on the patenting process, which can be of immense use to budding innovators.

Personally, it has been a very rewarding journey for me, because I learned something from each person I interviewed for the book.

I also thank my friends Ankit Mittal and Himanshu Gupta for their valuable feedback and my publishers for putting their faith in me.

Last, but not the least, I thank my parents, who have supported me through thick and thin. Their unquestioning support has been my pillar of strength.

Table of Contents

1   Anirudh Sharma – Haptic Shoe for the
               Visually Impaired   3

2   Hemanth Satyanarayana – Augmented Reality-based
               Virtual Trial Rooms   13

3   Mrinmayee Bhushan – Nanotechnology-based
               Herbal Hair
               Removal Crème   21

4   Shyam Vasudev Rao – Preventive Eye
               Care Device   31

5   Mansukhbhai Prajapati – MittiCool Refrigerator   41

6   Nelvin Joseph – Artificial Intelligence-based
               Power Saver   51

7   Nitin Joshi – Non-intravenous Chemotherapy   63

8   Prateek Bumb and Aniruddha Sharma
               – CO_2 Removal Technology   71

9   Priyanka Sharma – Ultra Low-Cost Immuno-
               sensor Biochip for Detecting
               Environmental Pollutants   79

10   Sachidanand Swami – Interactive Touch Surfaces   87

11   Sriram Kannan – Location Tracking
               without GPS   95

12   Abhijeet Joshi –Implantable Biosensor
                    for Diabetes Monitoring   107

13   Ganesh and Pragyanandesh – VORWIS   115

14   KK Plastic Waste Management – Road Construction
                                  Using Plastic
                                  Waste   125

15   Team Papyrus Efficiencia – Environment-
                              Friendly Paper   135

16   Science for Society – CareMother Testing Kit and
                          Digital Platform for Providing
                          Pregnancy Care   147

17   Chinmay Deodhar – Dual-Purpose Laparoscopic
                          Surgery Instrument   159

18   Arunachalam Muruganantham – Low-Cost
                                  Sanitary Pad
                                  Making Machine   169

19   Inncz – Offline Internet on Mobile Phones   181

20   IdeaForge – Netra UAV   193

Appendix

1   Patent and Prosper   205

Introduction

A discussion with an acquaintance in the US veered toward Indian engineers. My acquaintance stated that he respected Indian engineers, but didn't believe that any significant product-oriented research was taking place in India. There were no path-breaking, scalable products with global appeal coming out of the country, he said.

Over a period of time, I have realized that he is not alone in that belief. Many others are also skeptical about India's position on the innovation map of the world.

Undoubtedly, India lags behind several Western countries in innovation. According to the Global Innovation Index 2012, prepared by INSEAD in association with World Intellectual Property Organization (WIPO), India was ranked 64 among 141 nations surveyed. However, there is a growing tribe of men and women in the country who are devoted to product-oriented research with exemplary success.

In the process, they are also shattering the stereotypical image of Indian innovation, that of *"jugaad"*, that is, modifying or adapting Western technology to meet the demands of the price-sensitive local market.

Economic growth in a country usually leads to growth in innovation, as there is greater demand for better products and also greater competition to supply those products. As more players try to benefit from the existing opportunity, they are compelled to innovate in order to differentiate their products from those of their competitors.

Thus, economic growth leads to innovation and innovation, in turn, leads to further economic growth.

Unfortunately, our society does not encourage creative thinking to the same extent as in the West. Choosing an unconventional path is less likely to be appreciated. This attitude inhibits the process of innovation in our country.

In order to foster an environment for innovation, it is extremely important to highlight the success stories of innovators. This would help them garner much-needed attention and appreciation and also motivate the next generation to follow in their footsteps.

This book is a small effort in that direction. It chronicles the journey of a few innovators who toiled hard to make great products from scratch, despite facing greater challenges as compared to their western counterparts. This book is a celebration of their indomitable spirit.

The men and women featured in this book are from various parts of the country, belong to different age groups, have different educational backgrounds from PhD degrees to little formal education, and have worked in a variety of research areas. What unites them is their passion for what they are doing and their undying faith in their idea, despite numerous challenges. They represent a facet of new India – the India that refuses to accept defeat and is hell-bent on proving its potential.

Their stories also provide useful insights into the process of innovation – the challenges involved and the institutional support available in the country.

This book is a salute to the spirit and willpower of these innovators, and it will surely bring about a change in the innovation landscape in India.

"People who are crazy enough to think that they can change the world are the ones who do."

– Steve Jobs

Anirudh Sharma

Haptic Shoe for the Visually Impaired

When one thinks of an innovator, the image that comes to mind is of a dedicated, academically inclined person, following a planned path with clear goals. Nothing could be further from that image than Anirudh, with his boyish looks, cool hairstyle and flashy goatee, ready to venture into the unknown with fervent optimism and addictive zeal.

Anirudh was born into a middle-class family in Delhi. His father, a farmer's son, had migrated to Delhi from rural Rajasthan to obtain tertiary education. He was the first in his family to do so, and went on to become a professor at Delhi University. He has always been a strong influence in Anirudh's life.

Anirudh admits that he was a "troublemaker" since early childhood and always had an insatiable urge to know more about everything around him. He would often dismantle a working radio to find out who really made that noise? and earn the ire of his parents. He once used his compass to dissect a cockroach, because he wanted to see what a cockroach's stomach looked like and then terrorized his friends with the same. He was blessed with a creative mind, but would rather use it to plan the next big toilet bombing than toward cracking the next big exam. As can easily be guessed, this did not earn him any kudos from the teachers or the principal at school. Parent-teacher meetings were probably the toughest part of his school life, with an average report card and an above-average list of pranks to discuss.

The only thing he excelled at, while in school, was sports, especially cricket; he made sure that he got enough opportunity to play it via class bunks. Life was all good until Class X. For a change, he aced the Board exams, scoring a brilliant 89.6%, thanks to a few months of dedicated hard work and a strict mother. However, the real struggle started thereafter.

Anirudh reminisces, "I chose to get into the non-medical stream, which in India essentially means trying to get into the Indian Institutes of Technology (IITs), or at least into an engineering college. The increased work load and increased expectations about academic performance, coupled with peer pressure and the rashness of the late teens, led me toward desperation. I was hardly able to study or focus on anything. As a result, I failed in the class XI exams. My school gave me another chance, and luckily, I didn't screw it, though I barely managed to pass."

That was the bad patch in his life. His confidence was shattered and the people who cared about him were very concerned for him. He also gave up his dreams of clearing any entrance exam or achieving anything big in life, and found refuge in the rebellious world of Pink Floyd. He moved away from his erstwhile friends, who were still busy preparing for the coveted IIT Joint Entrance Examination (JEE), and instead, found company among people as aimless as himself.

"Looking back, even I do not understand what I was thinking at that time. Probably, that's what we call teenage."

Anirudh's life changed when he ventured out of home after Class XII, living independently for the first time. He rented a room in Jia Sarai, which is considered a den for people preparing for IIT and IAS exams in Delhi. Though he was supposed to be attending classes at Brilliant Tutorials to prepare for a second attempt at IIT-JEE, he only went for a couple of classes and then dropped out, without his parents' knowledge.

"In that despicable room, an archaic desktop was the only companion I had. Gradually, I developed a fancy for animation, largely due to the freelancing projects that earned me a decent amount of money to have an enjoyable life outside my parents' control.

Needless to say, I could not make it to IIT or any other godforsaken engineering college."

However, he continued with his effort for another year, with no success. Finally, the next year, his parents decided to enroll him in a nondescript engineering college under Rajasthan Technical University (RTU), near Bikaner.

"Life couldn't get worse. From the urban sprawl of Delhi to the deserts of Rajasthan, it was a culture shock for me. Moreover, getting back to attending banal lectures reminded me of the hated days at school."

Thankfully for him, the college did not have mandatory minimum attendance.

"I almost never crossed the 10% attendance barrier that I had set for myself!"

Going to RTU, however, turned out to be a blessing in disguise for Anirudh, for he forged new friendships that were to have a great impact on his life.

During the first year, he met Rahul Motiyar and Sudhanshu Gautam. While one was the son of a carpenter, the other was the son of a railway repairman; but more importantly, both were full of enthusiasm for learning technical stuff hands-on. "There was an instant chemistry between the three of us and we became a formidable team, with our complementary skill sets.

Together, we embarked upon the mission of mastering the touch user interface technology, which was relatively new at that time. We had a modest aim of putting up a good show at the technical events hosted by the premier technical institutions across the country."

The three friends named themselves "Team Sparsh" and the first success came soon. At the hardware design competition at BITS Pilani, the team won the first prize, beating teams from some of the most reputed campuses in India. "We won ₹ 30,000 as cash prize, a princely amount for us back then.

Obviously elated, we set higher goals and participated at IIT Kanpur's hardware competition. We stood first again, beating teams from across Asia this time!"

Team Sparsh then decided to collaborate with the Industrial Design Center at IIT Delhi to take the work on the touch user interface forward. "Those were heady days. I had to learn everything from carpentry to coding and electronics, but the thrill of doing something so unique took the fatigue away and it never felt like work. We were totally intoxicated with technology, so immersed in work that we didn't know the difference between day and night. I had become so obsessed with touch user interface devices that my friends started calling me "Touch Addict". In fact, that is still my identity in the world of blogs and tweets."

Anirudh also started conducting workshops in several colleges on Free and Open Source Software (FOSS) and founded the Linux User Group (LUG) in Rajasthan.

The work with touch devices and open source software led him to the Google Summer of Code (GSoC) program, a task-oriented summer internship where students were expected to complete a challenging open-source software project. During the program, he got the opportunity to work on Google SketchUp, a 3D modeling tool that was being developed by Google for design professionals.

"The money involved in GSoC is substantial, which is a good motivator. You get paid $5000 for two months of work! In fact, I got into GSoC for two consecutive summers and thoroughly enjoyed the experience on both occasions."

He was set to graduate by then, and to his parents' relief, landed a job too. This was no ordinary job, though, for he was picked to work at HP Labs, Bengaluru. It was a job that paid handsomely, and one he would have loved to do even for free. It also proved to be the next turning point in Anirudh's life.

"My manager was Sriganesh Madhavanath, popularly called SriG 'SreeJee', who is a Senior Research Scientist and the Principal Investigator for the Intuitive Multimodal and Gestural Interaction (IMaGIn) project at HP Labs, India. I learned a lot from SriG and he gave me complete independence to do things in my own way and at my own pace. I really appreciate SriG, because he could make a person like me work, no small feat given the fact that I am difficult to work with. It is usually my way or no way. At HP Labs, SriG showed enough trust in me and even allowed me to work on my own projects simultaneously."

It was here that the idea of a haptic (pertaining to the sense of touch) feedback-based shoe for the visually impaired took root in Anirudh's mind.

"I used to see visually impaired people daily in Koramangala, where I lived. One night, while staring at a new pair of Reebok shoes in my room, I thought, '*Hum inhen chalate hain, kya ye humen chala sakte hain?* (We make them walk; can they make us walk?)' It struck me that it was possible, if we could put sensors on the shoes along with four or more vibrators, each vibrating to indicate the direction in which one should walk.

Everything I needed to make this was available in the room. I immediately disassembled my Android phone and took out its vibrator. LilyPad, a wearable microcontroller, was lying in my cupboard. I assembled them, wrote a small code with Google App Inventor and conducted the first successful demo. It was seriously that simple."

While the initial design may have been that simple, months of work have made it much more complex and sophisticated now.

There are four vibration actuators on each side of the shoe and the interactions happen via a smartphone. The shoe works only with a smartphone as of now, but technology is being developed to enable interaction using a simple phone as well. You can voice input your destination into your smartphone. The phone then interacts with Open Street Maps via GPS, and gives directions to the device in the shoe via a wireless connection between the shoe and the phone. The directions are then relayed to the user via vibrations. The user needs to walk in the direction of the vibrating actuator – the left vibrators indicate a left turn and the front vibrators indicate walking straight ahead.

Further, there are proximity sensors to sense obstacles as far as three meters ahead. Unlike conventional GPS navigation, users can customize the path they want to take between any two points. This was an essential requirement, because the visually impaired may want to choose a smoother path – one with fewer obstacles – rather than the shortest path, or may want to follow the path they take every day, rather than the one indicated by the system.

The device is designed such that it can fit into shoes of any shape, size, material or design; and the shoes would not appear any different from those without the device. The device is also strong enough to withstand rough, day-to-day usage.

Anirudh has named his haptic shoe as *Le Chal*, which means "Take me there/Lead me" in Hindi. After months of painstaking development to add greater functionality and robustness, he tested the prototype on patients at LV Prasad Eye Institute in Bengaluru; the shoe was very well received.

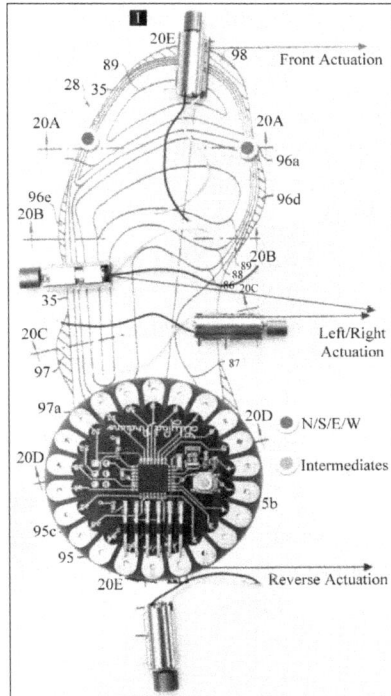

Design of *Le Chal*

In early 2012, Anirudh was named Innovator of the Year by MIT Technology Review in India for his haptic shoe technology. Many other awards and recognition followed. He was even invited to deliver a lecture at the TED event held at BITS Pilani (Goa campus).

Around this time, a common friend introduced him to Krispian Lawrence, an American patent lawyer. With Krispian's help, Anirudh worked toward patenting the technology. Together, they incorporated a firm named Ducere (meaning "to lead" in Latin) Technologies in order to develop a commercial version of the device.

"Soon, I decided to quit my job at HP Labs and work full time at Ducere. I moved to Hyderabad and another friend from college, Kunal Gupta, joined me to help with the electronics part of the device."

The bootstrapped company has been looking for the right investors.

"The shoe presents a big business opportunity, with an estimated 40 million people across the world affected by partial or full blindness. The cost of the shoe works out to be just a little over that of a regular pair of good shoes. Because blindness is not something that affects only the rich, affordability has been the prime concern during the design phase."

Anirudh's achievement has earned him more than just money, for he has gained admission to a fully funded master's degree program at MIT, and a chance to work with top researchers at the famed MIT Media Labs.

"I always felt that people from elite universities get special treatment and it is easier for them to attract attention. Thus, I feel MIT would give me what I missed due to (not clearing) the IIT entrance exam. It will be a great learning experience and networking opportunity. My partners at Ducere are committed to keep the work moving, despite my physical absence."

For the Innovator in You

"I would like to quote Richard Branson here: 'Screw it, let's do it!' Do not let your ideas remain ideas. Try them out without bothering about the consequences. Do not care about the naysayers; they will eventually be proved wrong when you are proved right."

Hemanth Satyanarayana

Augmented Reality-based Virtual Trial Rooms

Have you ever been frustrated by the long queue at the trial room of your apparel store? Or, do you find shopping online for clothes unreliable, because you cannot experience how the clothes would look on you?

Hemanth Satyanarayana has developed a solution for this – TrialAR or "Trial room using Augmented Reality", a technology that lets you try clothes digitally, without having to wear them.

In 2012, at the age of 29, Hemanth was named among the top innovators in India by MIT Technology Review. Though he started working on TrialAR only in 2010, his tryst with augmented reality dates back to his days at the State University of New York. Augmented reality (AR) is a term used to describe a combination of physical and virtual reality, in which our real-world environment is enhanced by computer-generated content.

Hemanth graduated from IIT Madras in 2003 with a degree in Mechanical Engineering and worked with IBM in software development for about a year. He then went to the US to pursue a Master of Science (MS) degree at the State University of New York (SUNY), Buffalo.

"During my IIT days, I was far away from anything related to innovation," Hemanth says. "I was very active in cultural activities and sports. I even served as the secretary of my hostel. As a result of these extracurricular engagements, academics remained low on my priority list."

It was during his MS that he was exposed to serious research. His MS was on virtual reality and allowed him to combine his software and mechanical engineering skills. As part of his thesis, he worked on augmented reality based open liver surgery.

"In this project, we took a 2D CT scan of the liver across various cross-sections and used them to generate a 3D model via computer graphics. The model was then put on special eyeglasses worn by the surgeon. The effect of each action of the surgeon on the liver was simulated and transmitted to the glasses in real time. This enabled the surgeon to ascertain what was happening inside the liver, without having to cut across various cross-sections to see that.

Augmented reality was in its nascent stages at that time and was increasingly finding new applications across industries. After graduating from SUNY, I joined a research based start-up called SoVoz, which was being run by a professor from University of Pennsylvania. I worked on the development of training simulators. SoVoz was a great learning experience, because it gave me exposure to many different technologies."

Hemanth got married in 2009. His wife, being a doctor, found it challenging to move to the US, because medical practitioners who obtain their education outside the US need to do a large part of their studies all over again in order to acquire a license to practice in the US. So, Hemanth quit SoVoz after almost three years and returned to India.

"At that time, I had no concrete plans. I had not looked for a job before returning to India and started thinking seriously about setting up something of my own. I met a lot of entrepreneurs in India during that period and figured out that entering the field of medical devices could be fruitful."

A friend introduced Hemanth to an interesting project at the Defence Research Development Organization's (DRDO)

Center for Artificial Intelligence and Robotics (CAIR). CAIR had developed a Laparoscopic Surgery Simulator to help doctors train for laparoscopic surgeries. Laparoscopy involves inserting two probes into the body, one for imaging and the other for conducting the operation. Doctors need very good hand-eye coordination for laparoscopic surgeries, because they have to operate on the body while looking at a screen. This simulator allowed them to practice in a virtual 3D environment.

After eight to nine years of research, DRDO was looking to sell off the technology to interested private players who could then commercialize it. Hemanth decided to enter the fray. He met the concerned people at CAIR and completed the formalities. However, several months passed, and despite visiting DRDO numerous times, he could not make any progress. After almost a year, having realized that the authorities had no serious interest, he decided to abandon the idea.

It was a tough period for Hemanth and people around him were getting anxious about his future. In 2010, he enrolled for a year-long post-graduate diploma in Intellectual Property Rights at NALSAR University of Law, Hyderabad. Simultaneously, he started work on a new idea – a gesture-based gaming application.

The application involved a camera to capture simple hand gestures and an LCD screen to project the pictures. The software generated random pictures and interpreted users' hand gestures. Users could swipe and select a picture, and the selected picture would break up into jumbled pieces. Users could then entertain themselves by arranging the jumbled pieces using hand gestures. Photoplay, as Hemanth called it, took about three months to develop, but unfortunately, it did not sell. "Even though it did not yield any positive economic results, it gave me hands-on experience in developing gesture-based user interaction." Thankfully, the experience wasn't wasted, as it led to something more interesting and meaningful.

"At a boutique one day, I realized that it takes a lot of time and effort for women to try on several saris before they purchased any. This is a hassle for both the customer and the store owner. I thought that AR could be used to superimpose the virtual collection of saris on the captured image of a customer, which could then be projected onto a screen for viewing. That would enable the customer to easily try the whole collection in a short time, by simply using hand gestures to change to the next outfit."

Learning from Photoplay's experience, this time, Hemanth did a thorough market research before embarking on the project. The product seemed to have good potential. In late 2010, he finally started working on TrialAR wholeheartedly. "I rented a small 100 sq ft office space and hired two eager-to-learn interns from an engineering college. The company, Imaginate, was formally incorporated in January 2011.

"The first prototype was ready by mid-2011 and we tried it at a boutique. Each outfit was put on a mannequin and the mannequin was pictured from a certain distance. The whole collection was similarly digitized. A 42-inch LCD screen was then put on a wall and a camera was placed at a suitable location to capture the customer's image and hand gestures. The system worked perfectly and the customers were quite delighted to use it.

Now that the system was tested, I started looking for investors to scale things up. However, I did not have any prior experience in doing that. It was also taking a lot of my time, which meant that further development of the product suffered."

At that time, Pawan Kosaraju, Hemanth's friend from IIT Madras joined the company. "He had faith in my idea and left his job at KPMG, Germany to come back to India and work with me. This eased the workflow."

After successfully creating the desktop version of the system for physical stores, the company started working on the web-based version for online retail stores. Several e-commerce firms expressed keen interest in the product, but the company did not want to roll the product out before perfecting it.

"We then developed a patented application for collaborative shopping, which allowed people to seek the opinion of their spouses and friends online, in real time, before they finalized their choice."

In November 2011, Imaginate was named among the Top 10 Product Companies in India by NASSCOM. In March 2012, it was selected as the Startup of the Year by the Indian Chapter of the Startup Leadership Program. Around the same time, MIT Technology Review named Hemanth among the top Indian innovators.

In June 2012, Imaginate was selected for Start-up Chile, a program by the Chilean Government to attract early stage, high-potential entrepreneurs. The government provides each selected start-up an equity free amount of $40,000 to bootstrap their start-ups in Chile and use it as a platform to go global.

"In August 2012, I travelled to Silicon Valley to explore possibilities and a lot of people showed interest in the technology. Qualcomm promised to fund us, if we could develop applications that enable the use of our technology via smartphones. So, that's the next step for us.

We are also improving the technology to enable better tacking – that is, enabling the clothes to move as the person moves. Currently, the technology does not take into account the body contours of the individual; thus, that is another area for improvement.

It may not completely replace the physical trial room, but it definitely enables you to reduce the number of choices that you would like to physically try out."

Imaginate estimates the market potential for TrialAR to be about ₹ 4000 crore (about $800 million) in India alone. They have been showcasing the technology abroad at fashion and technology events and have received favorable offers from some luxury fashion brands and online apparel retailers.

Besides TrialAR, Hemanth is also working on other products based on augmented reality.

"We have developed an AR-based smartphone app that has the potential to make every newspaper like the *Daily Prophet* of the *Harry Potter* series. You need to switch on the app, roll the camera of your smartphone over the headline and then hold the phone over the accompanying picture. The app will find relevant video clips on the internet and superimpose the video over the photo. You will thus read the article on your phone screen with the video playing inside the photo-frame. If you move your phone away from the newspaper, the video will resize to fit the frame of the photo; if you move the phone laterally, the video will adjust its position to still remain superimposed on the photo. So, on your phone screen, you will always see the text from the newspaper being captured by your camera and the video content generated by the app."

As Hemanth continues on his journey to bring fantasy to reality, or rather, augmented reality, this will be one of the many successes that are lined up for him.

For the Innovator in You

"Innovation is an uncertain domain. Be prepared for surprises, pleasant and harsh, especially harsh. Manage your personal finances such that you can afford a decent lifestyle within a small budget. This will help you weather the hard times better. Even after returning from the US, I chose to buy the value-for-money Tata Nano. This allowed me to channel most of my savings toward better uses. Being satisfied with your current level of material comfort is necessary to focus your intellectual energies on creative pursuits. Otherwise, your energies would be focused only on attaining higher material comfort."

Mrinmayee Bhushan

Nanotechnology-based Herbal Cream to Inhibit Hair Growth

Mrinmayee's journey towards innovation began when she enroled for an MSc (Microbiology) program at Pune University and started working for her thesis on Protein Synthesis Inhibitors. One of her female relatives suffered from abnormal facial hair growth and had to face embarrassment because of that. Mrinmayee began to wonder if the solution lay in protein synthesis inhibitors, whether they could be used to retard the growth of unwanted hair.

"Hair is fibrous protein that is produced at the hair root and pushed upwards through a tube," Mrinmayee explains. "When hair is removed by various shearing methods like shaving or waxing, a new hair strand starts to grow in its place. Therefore, regular shearing is required, which may be painful and time-consuming, and may also lead to rashes, skin loosening and other problems."

She adds that most permanent hair-removal methods, such as laser treatment and electrolysis, are very expensive and have side-effects. Moreover, these methods may not be equally effective for everyone, depending on their skin and hair color.

Furthermore, the topical (cream-based) products available in the market for hair removal may sometimes lead to skin darkening or thicker and faster hair regrowth. The chemicals in the creams may also cause allergic reactions in some people.

Mrinmayee envisaged a solution that would stop hair growth altogether, rather than just removing hair periodically. The solution would use naturally occurring ingredients, so that there were no side-effects, and would be affordable and easy to use.

After completing her MSc in 1994, Mrinmayee married Bhushan, a childhood friend. Bhushan, who is an engineer, had completed his MBA from Symbiosis institute of Business Management and was working as a Deputy Manager at Essar Steel. He encouraged her to keep working on her idea rather than take up a job.

"Bhushan has been my pillar of strength. I would not have been able to achieve anything without his support. Even in the most difficult times, he stood by me and had full confidence in what I was doing.

Though I continued my research and experimentation from my home laboratory, the pace was very slow. We had to keep moving to a new city every couple of years due to Bhushan's job. In this period, I also did a Diploma in Pharma Management, obtaining a gold medal. Meanwhile, we had two kids and other priorities of life took most of my time."

After four years with Essar Steel and another four with Tata Steel, Bhushan quit the steel industry to become a Director at the Indian operations of an Australian water treatment company. The family then relocated to Pune, which was of great help to Mrinmayee.

She got back in touch with her guide at University of Pune, who helped her connect with Dr Kishori Apte, an expert on animal testing at the National Toxicology Center, Pune. Dr Apte, who has 25 years of experience in toxicology and pharmacology and is also associated with the APT Research Foundation, Pune, helped Mrinmayee to further her research at the APT Research Foundation and carry out toxicology studies at the National Toxicology Center.

Mrinmayee worked toward formally incorporating her company, Mindfarm Novatech in 2003. The product was not ready, but the research work was in its final stages. She also met several experts in the pharmaceutical industry and explored various aspects of the patenting and commercialization process.

Initial toxicology and efficacy studies were completed in 2004 and Mrinmayee filed for her first patent in 2005 – an Indian patent titled 'Topical composition for inhibiting the growth of mammalian hair'.

"Unfortunately, our patent lawyers in India did not do a great job. That meant that I had to do a major part of the work, despite paying the hefty fee.

We then filed for a patent under the Patent Cooperation Treaty (PCT), which enables the innovator in any country to file for a single patent for protecting his/her intellectual property across multiple geographies.

If you are considering filing a patent application in five or more countries; if you intend to apply for foreign patents on your invention, but are not sure where; or if you will be applying for foreign patents, but would like to delay the substantial expense of filing many applications, you would be well advised to do your foreign filing through the PCT. You can then eventually file for country-specific patents, as and when required, for additional protection."

Mrinmayee's experience of filing for a US patent was nightmarish. "We hired an American patent lawyer, and filed for both the product and process patent together. The patent examiner called up the patent lawyer and asked which of the two should be processed first. Ideally, the lawyer should have consulted us before taking a decision, but he proceeded without doing so and chose the product patent. As it turned out, there existed some prior art on the product patent; thus, it was rejected. Patent lawyers are very expensive in the US; so, we lost a lot of money without any results to show for it."

Because funds were in short supply, the company had to abandon their plans for the Canadian and European patents.

"Some countries allow you to file the patent on your own, without going through a patent lawyer. I halted research work and devoted all my energies to studying the patent law. After that, I successfully filed the South African and Australian patents on my own.

In order to get some protection in Europe, we then decided to file a patent in the UK. We chose the UK, because we did not have to bear the expenses of a translator for filing the patent in the local language. Language is very critical in a patent. The way the idea is portrayed is almost as important as the idea itself."

In 2006, MindFarm launched the first version of its product, named Romantaque (pronounced as Rom-an-tak), which literally means something that puts an end to hair (growth). Bhushan and Mrinmayee were doing everything on their own so far, with Mrinmayee handling the technology and Bhushan handling everything else. Therefore, they decided to outsource the production to Sri Ganesha Ayurvedic Pharma, Pune. The distribution of Romantaque was awarded to a leading pharmaceutical distributor and the product was sold at various retail chains and pharmaceutical shops.

"The product received a very good response from customers. After using it, they came back for more. This confirmed the need for such a product and the ability of our product to meet customer expectations."

However, unanticipated problems with the distribution came up soon.

"We made a big mistake by awarding an exclusive distributorship. The distributor was not putting in enough effort to drive sales and the contract prevented us from using any other distribution channel. It was frustrating to see that despite demand from customers, the product could not reach them. As a result, we had to discontinue the sale of Romantaque after selling about 200 kg of the product.

We had invested a lot of our savings into the product. It was a big disappointment."

As they say, every dark cloud has a silver lining. The visibility from the launch of Romantaque got them an invitation to the Inventors of India forum at IIM, Ahmedabad, where they met Dr AS Rao from the Department of Science and Technology (DST). He urged them to apply for the Technopreneur Promotion Program (TEPP), but Mrinmayee was reluctant because she didn't trust government schemes.

"There is usually a lot of red tape. But we really needed money to take the work forward and the choices were few. So, we applied without much hope."

They turned out to be among the chosen few to receive the ₹ 10 lakh TEPP grant that year, with the first installment arriving in just four months. "It couldn't have been timed better. It saved us from a lot of financial trouble.

"We used the TEPP grant to further improve the product. In association with IIT Bombay, we developed a nanotechnology-based formulation for more targeted delivery of the plant extract to the hair follicle. We then filed for a new set of patents.

In 2009, we were invited for a conference organized by the The Indus Entrepreneurs (TiE). Some investors there showed interest in the technology and offered support for scaling it up.

There were very strong negotiations. We thought that instead of holding on to a small pie, we would be better off with a small piece of a much bigger pie. So, we bent to the pressure and gave away more than we should have.

Investors suggested that a new company be floated and the patents, which were in my name, should be transferred to it. Apart from investing the money, they were to add value via their contacts, experience and knowledge of the market. They also promised to bring in bigger investors for the second round of funding. However, things did not move at the anticipated pace.

A bigger investor did come in, but that proved to be our undoing. He initially offered to invest an additional ₹ 3 crore in the company, so that the product could reach the international market. However, just when the deal was in the final stages, he backed out, without even bothering to explain the reason.

Once he opted out, other investors followed suit and the company had to be closed down. Thankfully, the patents were yet to be transferred to the new company. So, at least our intellectual property was still unharmed.

We were planning to revive the process of filing for the US patent, but once again, we were short of funds.

DST came to our rescue once more in this tough time. We applied to the DST–Lockheed Martin India Innovation Growth Program in April 2011.

We were declared the winners and received a lot of media coverage. Through it, we got in touch with office-bearers at the Federation of Indian Chambers of Commerce and Industry (FICCI) and IC^2 Institute, an interdisciplinary research and technology incubation center of the University of Texas. They offered us help in finding a partner in the US. Thus encouraged, we started working toward launching the new, improved Romantaque by December 2011."

However, just when things were starting to look up, another tragedy shook their world. In July 2011, Bhushan met with a life-threatening accident when his motorbike was hit by a speeding car driven by an underage driver. Bhushan sustained serious head injuries and 36 fractures on his body. His rib cage was broken and lungs were punctured at several places. Fortunately, the site of the accident was near a hospital and he could get timely medical help.

"His good karma, prayers of well-wishers and his strong willpower saved his life. He spent about two months in the ICU and many more months for a complete recovery."

Because of the accident, Mrinmayee and Bhushan could not attend the expositions organized by the Lockheed Martin Innovation Growth Program to connect the innovators with experts, mentors and interested investors.

However, despite the physical, financial and emotional setbacks, they continued working, and finally, Romantaque was re-launched on July 1, 2012.

"Owing to our bad experience with the distributor earlier, we decided to use online retail channel this time and sell the product directly to users. Romantaque is now available for direct purchase at our website, www.romantaque.com.

Romantaque is the only clinically proven herbal product that inhibits hair growth," explains Mrinmayee. She mentions another clinically proven hair-growth inhibiting product, Vaniqa (pronounced as Van-i-ka), but says that unlike Romantaque, it is a chemical formulation. "Vaniqa can be used only on the face, not on other parts of the body. And unlike Romantaque, it does not work well for everybody."

Mrinmayee explains that Romantaque is very simple to use. It needs to be applied 24 hours after a hair-removal session (such as waxing or threading) and then twice a day for the next 10 days. "This should be done after every hair-removal session and results are perceptible after the second or third cycle. Fewer hair regrow and hair is shorter in length and thinner. As hair growth reduces, so does the pain involved in hair removal. Also, you do not need to go for hair removal as often.

Hair removal from the follicle, for example, by waxing, epilating, threading or plucking, opens up the orifice and exposes the hair follicles. When Romantaque is applied regularly, these follicles are either partially or completely deactivated, resulting in reduced or no regrowth. Romantaque can also be used if you shave or use depilation creams, but the effect is slower, as can be expected."

Mrinmayee shares her future plans. "We are bootstrapping and sales are gradually picking up. We hope to make it big this time."

Mrinmayee's story is a classic case of victory against all odds. The journey was long and arduous, but she did not give up. Her faith in her vision, and the ambition of turning it into reality, kept her going in the toughest of situations. She is indeed a great inspiration for all innovators and entrepreneurs.

For the Innovator in You

"It is very important to understand the patenting process. You cannot leave the protection of your idea to a patent lawyer, especially to one who may not be very competent. When you can develop a complicated technology with high commercial value, you can definitely understand patent laws. Nobody can present your idea better than yourself. You can also save a lot of money. So, it is totally worth the effort.

Do not be disheartened by bad experiences. Give hope half a chance and despair will not win. Your patience and perseverance will be tested, but you will eventually be a success if you keep treading your path."

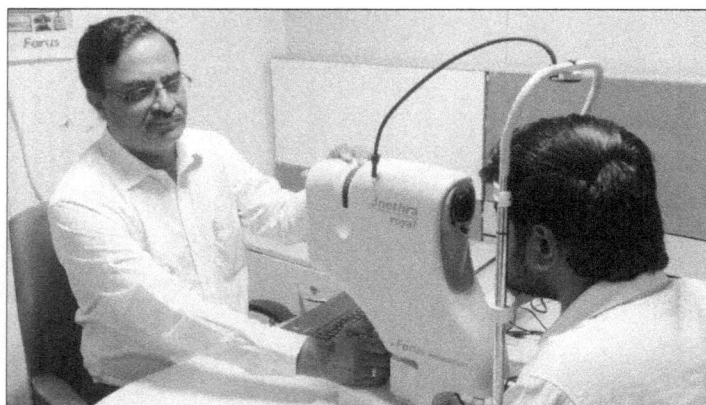

Dr Shyam Vasudev Rao testing a patient with 3Nethra

Preventive Eye Care Device

At the age of 50, Dr Shyam Vasudev Rao is a "serial innovator". An electronics engineer from Mysore, he completed his MS and PhD degrees at the Indian Institute of Science (IISc), Bengaluru.

His first brush with innovation and entrepreneurship was in 1988-89 when he built a virus-free card – a memory card that could be used to carry data and had the ability to resist a virus attack. He did not have any prior experience, inherited fortune or connections, but undeterred, he successfully manufactured and sold the card to vendors across the country.

Those were the days when India was a closed economy and imports were discouraged, because they drained precious foreign exchange. The government encouraged import substitution – developing products locally that could be used as substitutes for products that would otherwise be imported.

Dr Rao also worked on process automation (that is, developing and customizing machinery for production) for rubber, chemical, steel and other plants, and the business boomed.

By 1994-95, however, the business environment in India had begun changing. After economic liberalization in 1992, many multinational companies (MNCs) entered the Indian market and it became difficult for small players to survive.

At the same time, India started emerging as a hub for software exports and many MNCs set up shop in the country to develop software for overseas markets. The Swedish communications giant, Ericsson had just entered India and was looking to set up an R&D facility in Bengaluru. Shyam received a job offer from them and decided to shut down his business.

Given his prior experience with technology and entrepreneurship, he was given the task of setting up the whole R&D center, right from recruiting people to identifying products that could be developed.

"It was a very challenging role, but with the right support from colleagues, I was able to execute it to perfection," says Shyam. "In fact, within two years, Ericsson opened another center in Hyderabad and then another in Delhi. The employee strength went up to 600 in four years!"

Impressed with his performance, the bosses in Stockholm had him transferred to Sweden as a Strategic Product Manager. This proved to be a defining experience for him.

"I came across a very different way of life. For the first time, I was exposed to the process of developing products for the global market.

The Swedish researchers were never in a hurry to get results and analyzed problems in greater detail, as compared to their counterparts in India. As a result, the outcome was usually much better than what could be achieved in India."

Unfortunately, in the early 2000s, Ericsson ran into financial problems, and in 2002-03, closed their R&D centers in India. Shyam was looking to return to India for personal reasons and realized that he would not be able to remain with Ericsson. He decided to switch to Philips and returned to India as the Technical Director for Philips in India.

"I came back to Bengaluru in 2004 and set up the R&D facility for Philips in order to develop products for the Indian market per Indian needs. The research center was extremely successful, producing five patents in the very first year, 20 in the next year, eventually reaching one patent per five employees per year."

At Philips, Shyam got good exposure to medical devices and healthcare. In 2010, he quit Philips and set up Forus Healthcare, a company devoted to manufacturing low-cost preventive healthcare devices.

"A friend of mine from Philips, K Chandrashekhar (referred to as KC) joined to take care of the marketing, and thus, Forus was born. KC holds an engineering degree from BITS Pilani and an MBA from IIM Calcutta. He has extensive experience in the semiconductor industry and currently serves as the CEO of the firm, while I am the CTO.

Forus means 'for us', that is, healthcare for the masses – a sustainable system of healthcare provided for the community, by the community."

Shyam explains that the deplorable medical situation in the country was one his reasons for setting up Forus.

"There is just one doctor for every 2,000 people in India. This is one-third of the world average. For specialties like ophthalmology (medical specialty related to eye care), the ratio is as high as 1:14,000. Also, the cost of healthcare is very high."

Forus focuses on preventive healthcare, including everything from hygiene to regular screening for medical ailments. Shyam explains, "Most of the innovation in medical science is directed toward curative treatment. Preventive healthcare is much cheaper than cost of a cure (medicines, operation, doctor consultancy, diagnosis and so on).

At any given time, only 4% of our country's population has access (monetary and physical) to curative healthcare. However, if we can ensure that preventive healthcare reaches

100% of the citizens, we can reduce the need for curative healthcare.

In India, access to reliable electricity is still a big problem in most parts of the country. Yet, there are hardly any screening and monitoring devices that run on battery. Thus was born the idea of making portable medical devices that run on battery and can be carried from village to village.

We came across Dr Aravind of the world-famous Aravind Eye Hospital. Dr Aravind is a very inspiring personality. He told us about blindness in India and how his hospital was using innovative methods to reach the poor and reduce the cost of eye-care. It was overwhelming to see the hospital's services and its innovative business model that used doctors and equipment very efficiently."

According to statistics from the World Health Organization, someone, somewhere in the world becomes visually impaired every five seconds. India has the highest number of visually impaired people in the world – 15 million of the 40 million across the globe. Unfortunately, 75% of blindness cases in India are due to reasons that are completely avoidable. Screening for and diagnosing eye problems and providing care, however, comes with its own set of challenges.

Ophthalmology requires expensive equipment. Even for screening/testing alone, at least two devices are needed for the anterior part of the eye and two for the posterior part. The equipment is bulky and cannot be moved easily. Thus, the same equipment cannot be used at two separate facilities; each would need its own, even if they are not being used simultaneously.

Furthermore, the process of testing and analyzing the results is quite complex and time-consuming and requires trained paramedics and ophthalmologists. The patient's pupils often need to be dilated for screening, which again takes several hours for recovery. This is inconvenient and for a daily-wage earner, it may mean the loss of a day's wages. That is one reason many of them avoid going to hospitals for testing, until absolutely necessary. However, by that time, it is often too late.

Shyam says, "If the screening process is automated, the doctor's time can be used to look after only those patients who need his attention."

That is what 3Nethra is designed to do. "3Nethra combines all four screening devices into a portable, battery-powered device, which anybody can be trained to operate. The device does not require the pupil to be dilated. It takes the image of the eye, analyzes it and comes up with the diagnosis on its own, without the need for an ophthalmologist. The report can then be presented to the ophthalmologist, if consultation is required (that is, if the ailment is detected)."

While the four screening devices together cost ₹ 15-20 lakh, 3Nethra costs only ₹ 5 lakh. It consumes just 10 watts of power and can last several hours on a single charge. The testing procedure takes only about five minutes and can detect five eye ailments – cataract, glaucoma, diabetic retina, refraction problems and cornea problems – diseases that contribute to 90% of avoidable blindness in India.

About 20% of diabetes patients face the risk of losing their eyesight. This is called diabetic retinopathy or simply diabetic retina. This is a big challenge in India, because the country is home to the highest number of diabetes patients in the world. There are about 50 million diabetes patients in India, with another 30 million on the borderline. Thus, almost 80 million people need screening twice each year for diabetic retina alone.

"If detected at the right time, diabetic retina can be corrected to restore normal eyesight and regular diabetes treatment can limit any further damage. But many diabetics (especially those belonging to lower economic classes) do not even know they have diabetes. If they are screened regularly for eye ailments, their diabetic condition would be detected as soon as their diabetic retina shows up. Thus, they can be treated for both conditions."

Shyam reiterates how 3Nethra helps to optimize a scarce resource in India – ophthalmologists, especially those specializing in diabetic retina. "There are just 14,000 ophthalmologists in India, of which only 900 have expertise to handle diabetic retina. However, most of their time is wasted in looking after patients who can be helped by other ophthalmologists. Even these doctors want to treat patients who fall in their specific domain area, but are unable to reach out to them. With 3Nethra, it is possible. 3Nethra detects the problem and the report generated also suggests the nearest doctor who is capable of handling that problem."

Shyam is happy with the tremendous response to the device. "We have achieved 50 installations so far, in villages as well as cities. Even established hospitals like Saraf Eye Hospital, Aravind Eye Hospital and Agarwal Eye Hospital, have bought the machine. We have supplied the machine to six other countries too. We plan to sell 200 units this year and aim to reach a level of 10,000 units a year by 2017.

On a recent visit to India, the US Secretary of State, Mrs Hillary Clinton appreciated our work and said that this innovation is as useful in the US as anywhere else in the world. She has assured us full support in getting funding and regulatory approvals. We have already tied up with I²T Institute in the US for assistance in marketing our product in the North American market."

Apart from rural health, 3Nethra also takes care of rural employment. The business model empowers small rural entrepreneurs and creates a self-sustaining ecosystem around the device that would not require government subsidies.

"A two-month course trains any graduate to operate and maintain the machine. The person can then either purchase or rent the machine to be used in his village and surrounding villages. He can cycle to each village with the machine and conduct testing for the patients at their home, charging just about ₹ 50. We want to achieve true democratization of healthcare – affordable to everybody, provided to the community by the community members."

Developing 3Nethra has been challenging on many technical fronts. Since the medical devices industry is highly research oriented and expects huge profitability, even the most basic functionality in existing devices has been patented.

"We were trying to combine several optical devices into one. For this, we needed to split the light beam so that the same beam can be used for testing multiple things at the same time. Though there are several processes available for this, we had to struggle hard to find a unique way of doing it, so that none of the existing patents were infringed. Moreover, we had to do it in a cost-effective manner that allowed the device to remain portable. This was, by far, the most challenging part of designing 3Nethra."

The company, fortunately, received early angel funding and did not have to face many financial challenges; most of their challenges were on the technical side. The process involved a high level of R&D inputs and getting the right people was important. "We built a team of around 12 very competent researchers. Most of them had worked with me at either Ericsson or Philips and were passionate about what we were trying to do. We also tied up with IIT Kharagpur and IISc. We have recently managed to obtain a $5 million funding from Accel Partners and IDG Ventures India, two of the leading venture capital funds in the country."

The company has applied for seven patents on 3Nethra, the most important being the one on cornea imaging, retina imaging and refraction measurement via a single optic line. Besides that, there are patents on image processing and pattern recognition and on indirect measurement of physical parameters.

3Nethra has received due recognition, with the team winning several awards. In 2010, 3Nethra was awarded the Sankalp Award. The Department of Science and Technology (DST) conferred the Lockheed Martin Gold Medal upon it in 2011. The same year, it also received the Piramal Award, the Samsung Innovation Quotient Award and the Anjali Mashelkar Inclusive Innovation Award.

Shyam shares his future plans. "We are now working on another device, ROP (Retinopathy of Prematurity) machine." ROP affects prematurely born babies. The eye is the last organ to develop in the fetus, and sometimes, when a baby is born prematurely, the retina is not yet fully developed. In many such cases, the retina can grow unusually fast over the 3-6 weeks after birth. The disorganized growth of retinal blood vessels may result in scarring and retinal detachment, which, if not treated in time, can lead to blindness.

"We need to scan about 3-4 million prematurely born babies each year for ROP. You need a special, wide angle camera to do this. Only a couple of companies currently produce such cameras and they easily cost several crores each. There are just 30-40 such cameras available in India. The ROP detection device we are developing would be substantially cheaper and much easier to use than any other available right now. Since most of the premature births occur in hospitals, many hospitals have shown interest in the device.

The 3Nethra pediatric machine, designed for children in the age group of 3-8 years, is also in the pipeline. This is the age group during which the imaging system of the eye develops. Many eye ailments, like squint, develop during this age, but become observable only at a much later stage, when it is usually too late. It is easily treatable in the initial stages. Thus, this device would help in the timely detection of eye ailments peculiar to this age group."

An innovator once is an innovator for a lifetime. Shyam is a visionary with an inspiring passion for innovation and social good. We hope his work goes on to serve the masses across the globe.

For the Innovator in You

"The progress in 3Cs – communication, computation and collaboration – has made it much easier for people to acquire and share knowledge. With the emergence of new and fairer business models, there is renewed vigor around the world to innovate for the people at the bottom of the pyramid. It is an underserved market that innovators should focus on, to earn good financial returns as well as great satisfaction.

In India, companies in the service industry multiply their wealth very fast, but this does not happen for a product-based company. Market acceptance for a product may take time, so one should be patient. Also, financial resources must be managed such that you do not have to be in a rush to make money."

Mansukhbhai recounting his MittiCool story to foreign audience via an interpreter

MittiCool Refrigerator

Mansukhbhai Prajapati may be the most popular Indian innovator that you have never heard of. He is the poster boy of grassroots level innovators in India, and has been featured in almost every newspaper in India, in the *Harvard Business Review* and even on Discovery Channel and BBC.

Mansukhbhai comes from a traditional clay potters' family. He was born in Nichimandal village, in Morbi district of Gujarat's Saurashtra region. Morbi is known for its glazed ceramic tiles and has several kilns.

In 1979, Nichimandal was destroyed by floods and Mansukhbhai's father was forced to migrate to Rajkot, where he found work as a construction laborer for daily wages. Mansukhbhai was left behind with his grandparents in Wakaner, 70 km from Morbi.

At the age of seven, his marriage was fixed with a girl from a relatively well-off family. He continued to study, but failed his class X exams. His father then arranged for him to work in a brick kiln, but Mansukhbhai hated it because of the dust. Soon, he convinced his father to let him buy a push-cart to sell tea on the highway, just outside Wakaner, but the endeavor didn't last too long.

"I enjoyed being a tea-vendor, but I lived in the fear that my in-laws would see me and call off the marriage. I used to hide behind my push-cart whenever my in-laws passed by the highway. Though the business was doing fine, I didn't want to lose my bride-to-be for it."

One day, the owner of a factory that made red roof tiles came to his stall. As he was having tea, he asked Mansukhbhai if he knew any young boy of his age who may be looking for employment. Sixteen-year-old Mansukh almost screamed in excitement that he was available. Even before the factory owner could tell him what the job entailed or how much he would be paid, he had accepted it.

The job at the factory required staying 24x7 within the factory premises. Day-to-day activities involved looking after the security and counting the roof tiles before they were loaded on the truck. Sometimes, Mansukhbhai had to substitute for any laborer who would call in sick.

"I was paid ₹ 10 a day, along with meals and had the factory floor for a bed. For the next six years, I did every odd job at the factory, from repairing the machinery to making the clay and sweeping the floor."

In 1988, at the age of 22, he married the woman he was betrothed to. Later that year, he left the job at the factory and started a workshop for making motor windings, in partnership with a friend who knew a little about making motors.

"As it turned out, he knew very little. The first batch of motors burned up on their very first use at the factory that had ordered them." The business incurred heavy losses and had to be shut down after six months.

Mansukhbhai then started a shop to sell sweets and snacks (*bhajiya*). This venture too ended unsuccessfully within six months, leaving Mansukhbhai in deep financial trouble. He was forced to approach moneylenders.

"I asked a few *lalajis* for a loan of ₹ 50,000. Because I did not have anything to offer as security, they weren't so keen to lend, despite the high interest rate that they usually charged."

Somehow, the owner of the roof-tile factory came to know of his plight through one of the moneylenders Mansukhbhai had approached. "He told the *lalaji* about my honesty and even agreed to provide the backing for the loan in case of default.

He personally came to my house along with *lalaji* to give me the much-needed ₹ 50,000. However, I was away from home at that time, and my father, unaware of my financial situation, told them that we did not need to borrow money.

Later, *lalaji* agreed to lend me ₹ 30,000 at 18% interest, which I accepted."

With the money left after repaying earlier debts, Mansukhbhai purchased some land and decided to enter the family's traditional business of clay pottery. His father, however, was against the idea, because he knew that there was little money to make in this profession. Mansukhbhai stood firm, for he felt that "it was at least a stable business and required less capital to start."

He started making clay flat pans (*tawas*), but due to his inexperience, broke about 25,000 *tawas* in the first year and ended up with zero profit. However, things gradually started to change for the better.

By 1990, the family together made about 100 *tawas* a day, but the money they earned was barely enough for survival. Mansukhbhai wanted to scale up the business, but could not afford to hire additional labor. Therefore, he thought about making a machine to make *tawas*.

For about a year, he experimented with several dies and finally succeeded in making a press for manufacturing clay *tawas*. This was his first in a series of innovations. The production increased from 100 to 1,000 *tawas* a day. Where Mansukhbhai would earlier sell *tawas* going from one village to another on bicycle, he now hired an auto-rickshaw.

In 1992, Mansukhbhai introduced a new offering, a clay pot (*matka*) with beautiful colors and designs.

"People found the shape and designs of the *matka* so attractive that we would sell whatever we produced almost as soon as we reached the market."

Mansukhbhai's financial woes were now over, but he wanted to do something more than just making a living.

On observing that the pond water that the villagers drank was quite polluted and often led to sickness, he started thinking about making a pot that could provide purified water.

By 1995, completely on his own, he had made a clay filter with pores as fine as 0.9 microns. He put the filter between two clay pots to create a system that provided clean and cool water at a nominal price of ₹ 100.

The earthquake that rocked Gujarat in January 2001 also jolted Mansukhbhai's hitherto comfortable life. The earthquake, measuring 7.7 on the Richter scale, is estimated to have left 20,000 people dead and another 160,000 injured. About 400,000 homes were destroyed and 600,000 people were left homeless, with the economic loss billed at about $5.5 billion.

Since it was winter, Mansukhbhai had stocked 5,000 *matkas* for sale during summer. Where brick-and-cement houses could not withstand the earth's fury, the clay pots too were shattered within seconds.

A reporter passing through Wakaner saw the pile of shattered *matkas* and clicked a few pictures. On February 26, 2011, exactly a month after the earthquake, a leading Gujarati daily, *Sandesh* carried the pictures on the first page with a caption that translates to "Poor man's refrigerator shattered".

This set Mansukhbhai thinking about making an actual refrigerator for the poor.

"*Matka hi garibon ka fridge hota hai. Gareeb logon ke paas fridge khareedne ke paise nahin hote, na hi usse chalane ke liye bijli ka bill dene ki kshamata. To maine socha ki kyun na mitti se aisa fridge banaun jo sasta ho aur bijli ke bina chale.*" (The clay pot is a refrigerator for the poor. They do not have the money to buy a refrigerator; nor can they afford to pay electricity bills. So, I thought, why not make a clay refrigerator that is cost-effective and works without using electricity.)

He decided to use the principles employed daily by vegetable vendors in India. During the summer, these vendors cover their vegetables with a wet cloth and keep sprinkling water over it. Evaporation maintains a cooler and stable temperature beneath the cloth and keeps the vegetables fresh.

Meanwhile, a newspaper reporter wrote about Mansukhbhai's effort to make the clay refrigerator. The news spread like wildfire, and soon, various newspapers were talking about this unimaginable endeavor. People started visiting Mansukhbhai and enquiring about the progress, though in reality, little had been achieved. However, this increased Mansukhbhai's resolve to realize his dream project. There were several failed attempts, each costing a lot of money.

"After the earthquake, the Gujarat government started giving loans to people to start new businesses, so that more people would get employment, which would help to restore normalcy in Gujarat. I applied for a loan of ₹ 7 lakh and it was approved. I put all the money toward making the refrigerator, but it still did not reach the required level of cooling. In order to pay the interest on the loan, I had to sell my house. I then sold my push-cart and a few other possessions as well. People started calling me mad.

Then, a miracle happened. Prof Anil Gupta of IIM Ahmedabad heard of my story and came to visit me. He was impressed with the refrigerator and invited me to come to Ahmedabad.

Mujhe laga ki koi loan *dila denge, to socha ek baar jaate toh hain Ahmedabad, shayad kuchh kaam ban jae. Par jab main Ahmedabad gaya to unhon ne mujhe GIAN waalon se milaya.*" (I thought he would help me get a loan. So, I thought of going to Ahmedabad to see if anything useful could come of the visit. But when I went there, he arranged for a meeting with GIAN.)

GIAN, or Grassroots Innovation Augmentation Network, is an incubator of grassroots innovations and traditional knowledge. GIANs have been set up at Ahmedabad and Jaipur to provide incubation support to grassroots innovators in West and North India, respectively. GIAN cells are also present at Tumkur and Madurai in South India, Kashmir University in J&K and the Sikkim Manipal Institute of Technology in Sikkim. GIAN works in association with the National Innovation Foundation (NIF), Honeybee Network and SRISTI (Society for Research and Initiatives for Sustainable Technologies and Institutions). These organizations share the common purpose of supporting rural innovation.

At GIAN, the manager offered ₹ 2 lakh to Mansukhbhai to support his work.

"*Maine bola ki main zyada byaaz nahin de sakta, to unhon ne kaha ki maine byaaz kab maanga. Ye do lakh rakh lo. Agar fridge achha ban jae aur bikne lage to wapas kar dena, nahin toh koi baat nahin hai. Main to hairan ho gaya. Aise paisa kaun deta hai, koi paper bhi nahi sign karaya. Main toh bahut khush hua. Woh toh bhagwaan banke aaye the mere liye!*" (I said I would not be able to pay a high interest. He replied that he wasn't asking for interest. He wanted me to keep the money and repay it only if the refrigerator becomes a success, otherwise not. I couldn't believe it. Who lends money like that! He didn't even make me sign any papers. I was very happy to receive the money. He came into my life like God.)

After experimenting with several clays and designs, Mansukhbhai finally completed the refrigerator to his desired perfection in 2004, and applied for a patent through GIAN. The refrigerator contains a water tank with a capacity of 10 liters. Through this tank, water percolates into spaces around the vegetable compartment. As it comes into contact with the air and evaporates, both the vegetable chamber and the remaining water are cooled. The water tank has a tap through which one can get the cool water. Moreover, the temperature maintained in the vegetable compartment is 10-15 degrees centigrade lower than the ambient temperature. Fruits and vegetables stay fresh up to five days, while milk lasts up to two days. The refrigerator can store up to 5 kg of fruits, vegetables, milk and other products. Because it does not cool to near-zero temperatures, fruits and vegetables retain their taste and nutrition, unlike in the electric refrigerator. Needless to say, this refrigerator is free from all CFCs (chlorofluorocarbons), the environmentally harmful gases used in conventional electric refrigerators as refrigerants. This eco-friendly refrigerator, aptly named MittiCool, costs only about ₹ 3,000.

GIAN helped Mansukhbhai get a trademark for MittiCool and set up a company by the name of Clay Creations. GIAN also helped him set up a website and engaged NID (National Institute of Design, Ahmedabad) to help him create attractive packaging for MittiCool. Today, Mansukhbhai sells his eco-friendly refrigerator to people in several countries across the world.

This serial innovator then chanced upon his next.

"In 2005, my wife asked me to buy a non-stick pan for her. I found that it costs ₹ 450. I did not want to spend that much, so I learned how to coat the non-stick material and started making my own non-stick pans.

I applied Teflon coating to my clay *tawas* and sold them for just ₹ 25. I also designed a metallic support for the *tawa* to prevent breakage during daily use and later added a handle for ease of use."

He applied for a patent for the non-stick clay pan in 2006. The next year, he participated in the annual food festival,

Saatvik, at IIM Ahmedabad to showcase his kitchenware. On seeing his range of clay kitchenware, one of the visitors approached him with a suggestion to make a clay cooker.

"Hamare purvaj mitti ki haandi mein khana banate the, toh khaane ka tatva bacha rehta tha. Aajkal ke bachhon ko itni jaldi chashma lag jata hai, logon ke baal jaldi safed ho jaate hain, kyunki khaane ki paushtikta ghat gayi hai." (Our ancestors cooked in clay pots, which retained the nutrition in food. Today, children begin wearing spectacles at an early age and many people have prematurely graying hair, because the food we eat is less nutritious.)

In 2009, I made a cooker out of clay. A laboratory in Mumbai conducted experiments on the nutritiveness of food cooked in a steel cooker and my clay cooker. It was found that *urad dal* lost 70% of its nutrients after cooking in a steel cooker, while what was cooked in the clay cooker retained 100% nutrients even after 36 hours."

Mansukhbhai has also made a thermos out of clay. His next aim is to make a clay house that would maintain a

MittiCool non-stick pan, cooker and hot case

constant temperature of about 20 degrees without needing any electricity. Cooling would be through water and air, while lighting would be natural or stored solar energy. He is also considering making small MittiCools, which he calls Minute MittiCools, capable of cooling water within five minutes. A German home-appliances company has shown great interest in his products. He has also received several other offers for collaboration.

He is an extremely busy man and is found delivering lectures at conferences, when not working on his new ideas at his workshop-cum-lab. He has delivered an INK talk and has been featured at a conference held at the Judge School of Business, University of Cambridge, UK.

Mansukhbhai has been honored with the title of "True Scientist" by Dr APJ Abdul Kalam. President Pratibha Patil awarded him the Grassroots Innovator Award. He has 25 other national awards to his name. He counts Prime Minister, Shri Narendra Modi among his customers and has been promised every possible support by him. *Forbes* magazine has named him "India's Most Powerful Rural Entrepreneur" while National Geographic called him "NatGeo Eco Hero."

For the Innovator in You

"*Bas apna kaam karte raho, himmat mat haaro. Kitni bhi mushkil aaye, peechhe mat hato. Jab aap koi achchha kaam karte ho, to phir use aage le jaane ke liye bahut se acchhe log mil jaate hain.*" (Do your work and do not lose heart. Whatever difficulties come your way, do not give up. When you do good work, you will definitely find good people to help you out.)

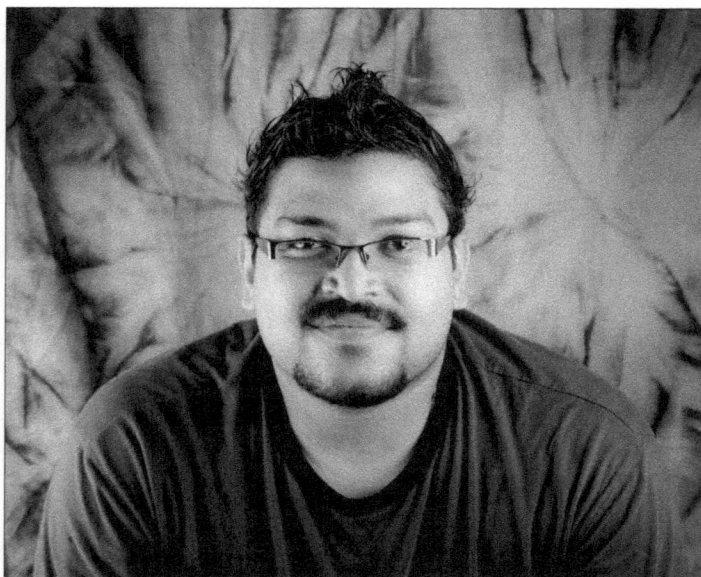

Nelvin Joseph

Artificial Intelligence-based Power Saver

Nelvin, who describes himself as a happy-go-lucky nerd, had his first brush with computers in Class IV, when his dad took him to his office. Inquisitive by nature, he quickly developed a keen interest in computers and approached a computer training institute near his home, in order to learn more.

At the institute, he came across a course on C (the programming language). He thought that with such a simple name (just one character of English alphabet), the course would be very basic and easy. He decided to get enrolled, but the institute stated that he was too young for the course.

Given his curiosity, he would not take no for an answer and convinced them to let him attend the classes. Within a few months, at the age of eight years, he was a diploma holder in computer programming using C language!

Thereafter, Nelvin had to move to a hostel as his parents decided to admit him to a Sainik school. At his new school, he met some of the best teachers he has ever had. The love for books led him to spend most of his free time in the school library. The librarian grew so fond of him that he used to procure books just for Nelvin.

"Usually in Sainik schools, most people are actively involved in sports and other extracurricular activities. But I was always surrounded by books. My classmates used to jeer at me and I did not have any good friends at school.

That made me create my own world – a world in which I could let my imagination loose. It also taught me not to care about what other people think or say about me."

During his early teens, he got to see the super-hit Holly-wood movie, *The Terminator*. That sparked his interest in robots. Thanks to his resourceful librarian, he started reading more about robotics. That was his first introduction to Artificial Intelligence (AI).

After school, he decided to pursue Electronics Engineering and joined an engineering college in Thiruvananthapuram.

"At college, I was very active in various technical activities. I used to manage the computer labs, organize events for various technical clubs and represent the college at programming competitions. I was a very active member of the IEEE (a global organization that supports activities related to electronics and electrical engineering) chapter of my college.

The higher education system in India is so rigid that it does not reward you for anything except your performance in a few exams related to the courses prescribed for your degree. So, even when I was heavily involved with technical activities at college, I was never among the toppers."

The academics of his course did not interest him. "Engineering courses are very theoretical and outdated. The teaching is usually uninspiring and there is hardly any hands-on work involved. This inhibits learning and crushes creativity. I used to hate the curriculum in college."

Nelvin gave vent to his creative energy via high-adrenaline gaming. He was a very active gamer and his passion for gaming earned him the nickname, Ninja.

His other passion in college was biking. "I was so crazy about bikes that I knew the technical specifications for each of them. I purchased an old Avenger for ₹ 7000 and modified it, designing and fitting all the parts myself. I even added a GPS, an audio kit, rear wheel disc brakes and an anti-lock braking system. The bike was extremely powerful.

I even drove it all the way to Kanyakumari with a group of biking enthusiasts from Kerala."

After completing the undergraduate degree, he wanted to go abroad for an MS degree in Applied Artificial Intelligence. He obtained admission to the University of Edinburgh for the course, but an unfortunate accident in 2007 prevented that dream from becoming reality.

"The night before my final college exam, I was studying with some of my friends. Late at night, we felt like having some light snacks and ventured out. I was the pillion rider on a friend's bike. Unfortunately, our bike hit a pothole in the road and I fell off, sustaining serious injuries. As a result, I could not appear for the exam the next day and my graduation was delayed. That put paid to my plans for the MS degree. The next best thing I could do was to get a job and that's what I did."

Nelvin joined a call center, across the road from his home, while he was still recovering. After his recovery, he joined Dell in Bengaluru.

"Though the pay was decent, it wasn't very exciting. I strongly felt that the job did not allow me to use my capabilities well. It was a routine hardware engineer's job. After a while, I decided to quit and come back to Kerala.

I came back home with no concrete plans. I wanted to learn AI in greater detail in my MS, so that I could eventually start my own company in the AI domain. I thought, why not do that now, rather than later? There are enough free resources available on the internet to learn from." He decided to start a company and use the internet to learn about product development and marketing.

Nelvin knew that his strong technical skills would not be enough for the company he envisaged. He also needed people with complementary strengths and the passion to start a business. He approached his friends and asked them to connect him with the people they knew.

"I gathered a team of six people, including myself. We rented a small house on the outskirts of the city to use as our first office. We had no products and no idea about what we should be making. The company was yet to be registered. We started brainstorming for ideas, but for several weeks, we could not come up with anything that would be commercially viable."

One day, when returning home, Nelvin realized that he needed a document that was stored on his office computer, but there was nobody in the office to email it to him. That made him think of developing a product that could switch devices on and off remotely, but further research showed that such products already existed. However, during his research, Nelvin chanced upon the concept of phantom power.

"All electronic devices, including computers, consume power when they are in standby mode. The power consumed in the standby mode is called phantom power. This power consumption leads to around 26% of the total wastage of electricity globally, and 57% of these losses are from computers alone.

Electricity is largely produced by using fossil fuels. Thus, we are contributing to global warming even when we are not using our devices."

Nelvin realized that a lot of electricity wastage in offices was due to negligence, which contributed to high costs for the organization. A power-saving solution based on artificial intelligence seemed to be a commercially viable venture.

According to a report by the US Department of Energy, 90% of users do not switch off their office computers while leaving for lunch or at the end of the workday. On an average, almost 100 kWh of power is wasted per computer per year because of this negligence. For a big corporation (with about 50,000 computers), this can mean an avoidable expense of over $1 million and reduction of up to 30,000 tons of carbon emissions.

"The cost of the wasted electricity can be as large as 3% of the total operating costs for some companies. Thus, reducing this wastage and saving costs can improve their competitiveness and also boost their green image," Nelvin adds.

"Soon after realizing the commercial potential of the idea, I started working on the technology. Meanwhile, a lot of people told me that I was extremely stupid to have left a good job to try idiotic things. Not many people showed faith in my ability or my idea."

Artin Dynamics was formally incorporated on April 15, 2008. Shortly after incorporation, Artin (short form of "artificial intelligence") found a place in the technology business incubator, Technopark in Thiruvananthapuram. Established in 1990 by the Government of India, Technopark is one of the leading technology incubators in the country, providing office space at subsidized prices and other support services such as helping ventures with marketing and brand promotions, investor relations, global exposure, etc., in exchange for a very small stake in the company.

"When we first approached Technopark, we didn't even know what a business plan meant. The Technopark authorities wanted us to write one, so that they could evaluate us. Fearful of revealing too much information, we wrote a few pages about artificial intelligence in general and the phantom power loss due to negligence. It contained no information on the technical details of the product, what it does and how it does that, how we planned to market it and what our revenue projections were."

Needless to say, the application was trashed. "We were then counseled by the Technopark consultants on how we should go about preparing our business plan. We were surprised to hear that we were required to estimate the revenues for the next five years. We wondered how we would come up with such hypothetical numbers when product development was yet to be completed and there had been no validation of market demand. But the consultants were impressed by the idea and were convinced about its market potential.

With their help, we worked day in and day out to develop a satisfactory business plan. The revised plan was accepted by Technopark and we got incubated within a week. This process usually takes about 8-10 months; we have been the fastest company ever to do it."

Artin began in a four-seat space. Within two months, it moved to an office with eight seats; and then to 16 in another two months, as new employees continued to be added. Most of the effort during this time was spent on product development. By the end of 2008, the company was ready with the first version of the product, meant only for computers.

Nelvin shares the story of how the product was named. "We were looking to give it some fancy name, yet something that represents what it is – a green technology which saves power. We started translating words like "green," "save" and so on, using Google Translator into several languages. After several iterations, we chose SPARA, which means "save" in Swedish.

SPARA is a software that can be installed on any computer. It studies the behavior of the user to recognize his usage pattern and then automatically implements power-saving actions.

For instance, if a user takes a lunch break between 2:00 PM and 2:30 PM for about 30 minutes, SPARA would be able to recognize this pattern and automatically save and switch off the monitor when inactivity is observed around 2:00 PM. The processor will not shut down completely, as the user is expected to return soon. The user can also override it if he returns sooner, or if he wishes to set up a software response on his own. Similarly, if the software observes that the user usually leaves the office at around 6 PM, then it would automatically save and shut down the system when it observes inactivity around that time."

Nelvin explains that SPARA is more effective than the power management system built into the computer. "If you set the computer to go into sleep mode after five minutes of inactivity is observed, it would do so, regardless of the situation. So, even if the inactivity is because the user is talking briefly to his colleague, the computer would be in sleep mode. This can get frustrating. In short, the piece of software built into the operating system is not *intelligent* enough to understand and interpret situations and adapt to human behavior. Even if there is a change in behavioral pattern due to a different user using the device, or the same user altering his habits, SPARA learns and implements the changes fast.

SPARA is four times more effective in reducing the daily power consumption of a computer, as compared to Windows Power Management. It has been observed that SPARA can help to save as much as 30% of the electricity that would otherwise have been used, which is almost three times of what could be saved by using Windows Power Management. It is as good as saying that if you use SPARA on three computers, you run the fourth for free. Usually, the investment on the device is recovered within two years."

Regarding competition, Nelvin states that a UK-based company offers similar solutions, "but its product is not as effective as ours.

"Because our technology is superior, we had little difficulty finding customers. In fact, usually customers find us, rather than we having to find them."

The big break for Artin came in 2009. As recession was looming large and companies were looking to cut costs, *The Economic Times* published an article on how SPARA could help companies cut expenses without reducing their employee count. Features in several newspapers followed. "The result was that, while several other established companies and start-ups were struggling during recession, Artin Dynamics grew rapidly.

Initially, we were looking only at the domestic market, but we soon realized that Indian companies are almost always reluctant to experiment with new technologies. Even if they can see good economic potential, they usually wait till the technology is proven abroad. So, we decided to focus on international markets first and wait for the domestic market to mature."

Artin filed nine Indian and foreign patents during this period. "Our patent lawyers did a good job, so we did not have any troubles with the patenting process," Nelvin adds.

"By early 2010, we were 30-employee strong and needed even bigger space. Technopark decided that we no longer needed the incubation."

Artin then rented a 6000 sq ft office within the Technopark complex. "Buoyed by the enthusiasm, we rapidly started scaling up and looked for a distributor for our products." However, a big setback followed.

"We received a big order for 1,000 pieces, but it turned out to be a big mistake. Without doing a thorough background check, we started processing the order. We spent a huge amount of money on the hardware and manpower. However, when the order was completed, the buyer reneged on his promise and we were left with 1,000 customized pieces which could not be sold to anybody else. The suppliers refused to take back the parts and everything was now as good as scrap.

My father trusted me with all his savings to meet the working capital requirements. My mother also pitched in by selling some of her jewelry. The company managed to stay afloat, but we couldn't pay the employees for several months. They cooperated and I cannot thank them in meager words for the confidence they showed in the company. We couldn't even pay the office rent to Technopark during this time, but they too stood by us in this tough time.

Just when we started to lose hope, a friend connected me to an investor from the Middle East who saw the potential and immediately poured in the funds." The funding came in toward the end of 2010.

In 2011, the World Bank chose Artin Dynamics as one of the 50 most innovative start-ups in the world.

The company has grown significantly since then, increasing its product portfolio under the brand name SPARA and appointing distributors in the UK, USA and Middle East, with plans to start operations in Australia soon.

The SPARA range includes specific power-management products for various devices. "For example, in an office, the water cooler would be used more frequently during the office hours, with low usage in the morning and peak usage around lunch time. However, even when water consumption reduces, the compressor may kick in regularly to maintain a certain water temperature. Say, it kicks in five times per hour during peak hours when more tap water needs to be cooled; reducing to two kick-ins per hour during non-peak hours and one per hour when it is idle. However, the compressor would not completely stop working unless you plug out the water cooler, which people rarely do. So, it will keep consuming power, even when cold drinking water is not required because there is nobody in office. A custom-made SPARA device can be installed to monitor the usage pattern of the water-cooler (via the number of times the compressor kicks in). Once the device learns the usage pattern, it will automatically cut off the power as required."

Nelvin sums up his journey so far as difficult. "Our experiences show that westerners find it very difficult to trust the quality of products made in India. They have little faith in the R&D capabilities of Indian companies.

The bias can be so strong at times, that Indian companies may feel a better way of gaining customer confidence is to pretend that the technology was developed abroad by their subsidiaries.

The prejudice is all the more pronounced for a company coming out of Kerala, which is known more for its backwaters, scenic beauty and herbal treatments than for engineering. We had to hire a European PR agency to spruce up our image."

Nelvin states that Artin's future plans include "conquering the gaming and mobile telephony space with AI-based products. It is difficult to reveal anything more at this stage. For the moment, the focus is completely on SPARA. There are millions of computers across the world, and thus, a huge market for it. We are working with Intel to customize SPARA for their new processor, VPRO.

We also plan an AI-enabled ATM machine, which will have the ability to read checks. So, you can just take a check that your employer issued and get cash directly."

For the Innovator in You

"The social pressure to conform is the biggest problem that inhibits innovation in India. People will tell you that what you are doing is plain stupidity. They will behave as if they know more about you and your work than you do. Eventually, the innovator loses confidence in what he is doing and gives up. Do not let this happen to you. Simply avoid such negative people.

If you are able to handle such people successfully, you will probably be able to achieve success with your product as well.

When I started Artin Dynamics, people who did not even know the first thing about artificial intelligence told me that 'such things' fail. Now, many of the same people come to me for advice.

I am a strong believer in destiny. Had I not fallen off the bike, probably I would have been in the US and would not have done what I did. Take your chances; you never know what destiny has in store for you."

Nitin Joshi

Non-intravenous Chemotherapy

Nitin Joshi lost his father when he was in class VII. His mother has been his pillar of strength. Born in Almora (Uttaranchal), Nitin was brought up in Haldwani, where he was always among the school toppers. Unfortunately for him, he could not clear the IIT-JEE and in 2002, landed up at the Kumaon Engineering College in Dwarhat, Almora.

"Since my ranking was not good enough to get me the much desired Computer Engineering course, I settled for Biochemical Engineering. I told myself that with a good standing in the first year, I would be able to switch to Computer Science the next year."

Over the next two semesters, he discovered that his passion for Computer Engineering was more "*bhed-chaal*" (herd mentality) than anything else, and that he was genuinely interested in Biochemical Engineering. Despite topping his class that year, he decided not to opt for the shift to Computer Science. Who would have known then that Computer Science's loss would eventually prove to be Biochemical Engineering's gain!

"At the end of my four-year engineering degree, I was awarded the Chancellor's Gold Medal by the university. I also secured AIR-31 at the competitive GATE exam (the Graduate Aptitude Test in Engineering is an entrance examination for admission into science and technology postgraduate programs in IITs and other Indian institutions and universities)."

Despite an outstanding academic record, Nitin did not apply to universities abroad, because getting a scholarship for a master's program there would have been tough. Besides, his mother wanted him to be in India, as she would be all alone otherwise.

"I got an admission call from both IIT Kharagpur and IIT Bombay. I chose the latter, because I thought it was better to be in a big city. But unfortunately, I did not manage to get a scholarship at IIT Bombay.

I still went ahead with the decision. I thought I might manage to get the scholarship eventually, if a couple of people chose to drop out of the program."

Fortunately for Nitin, two people dropped out by the time the session started and he obtained full scholarship for his MTech at the Biomedical Engineering Department.

"Biomedical engineering is very different from bio-chemical engineering that I had studied till that point of time. Biomedical engineering is more about human physiology, of which I had no idea when I started.

For my thesis, I chose to work with Prof Rinti Banerjee, who has a reputation for the quality of research pursued at her lab." She has an MBBS and a PhD degree in biomedical engineering, and was a fellow at the Cardiovascular Research Institute, University of California in San Francisco before joining IIT-B.

The credit for my initial pedagogy in physiology goes to Prof Banerjee, who has been a very able guide. I did not have any research experience before joining IIT, but gradually developed a knack for it. The research facilities at IIT were top notch and Prof Banerjee motivated me. Though I topped the MTech program with a CGPA of 9.8/10.0, my real joy was working independently at the lab."

After completing the MTech program, Nitin had a few tentative offers from top universities in the US, including MIT, for their PhD program. However, he was very comfortable with the academic atmosphere at IIT and the infrastructure at his lab matched the best in the world. Eventually, he decided to continue work on his PhD at IIT-B, under the guidance of the same professor.

"During the MTech program, I had worked on engineering inhalable nanoparticles capable of delivering a single anti-cancer drug, an innovation for which I obtained a patent in 2008. In the PhD program, I continued my work on non-invasive, targeted anti-cancer drug delivery. I extended the scope to engineer nanoparticles capable of delivering two different drugs and allowing for controlled release."

Nitin summarizes the status of current research in engineering nanoparticles for non-invasive anti-cancer drug delivery via the respiratory route. "Similar efforts have been attempted by several other research groups across the world, such as one at Rutgers University, where scientists synthesized inhalable silica nanoparticles. However, none of the nanoparticles synthesized so far have been commercialized, as serious problems have been found with each of them.

"Silica or polymer-based nanoparticles have been observed to induce a strong immune response, as they are alien substances for the body. In many cases, they even have very toxic side-effects. Most of them cause severe respiratory disorders, such as Acute Respiratory Distress Syndrome, which leave the patients gasping for breath. These foreign nanoparticles destroy pulmonary surfactants in the lungs, making it difficult for the lungs to contract.

Thus, our focus was to develop nanoparticles that are very similar to the naturally occurring pulmonary surfactants."

Nitin shares more details about his research. "After exhausting several possibilities, we tried to synthesize the nanoparticles to carry drugs by using the lipids that exist naturally in our body. Each of these nanoparticles had the shape of the number '8'. Thus, it had two compartments, one for each drug and a diameter of about 100 nanometers.

While engineering the nanoparticle, the shape and size were as important as the material. If not engineered with the right aerodynamics, the nanoparticles could get exhaled or may not go inside the nostrils at all when inhaled.

The combination of cancer drugs that we used – Paclitaxel along with Curcumin – was an unconventional choice. In fact, my guide was initially not too happy with the choice of drugs. Paclitaxel is one of the most popular and potent anti-cancer drugs. Curcumin, on the other hand, is a naturally occurring phenol in turmeric, which is responsible for its yellow color. Several medicinal properties of turmeric have been known to Indians for ages and it is used extensively in traditional Indian medicine. Unfortunately, the results have not been documented anywhere. Many foreign researchers are now trying to document the medicinal properties of Indian herbs. It's a pity that Indian researchers are yet to focus on their traditional knowledge.

My guide was of the view that pharmaceutical companies would not be interested in a product where the molecule employed is not widely accepted as a drug.

However, through my research, I had identified that Curcumin had excellent anti-cancer properties, and when used in combination with Paclitaxel, it increased the drug's efficacy and suppressed its negative side effects.

I was thus able to convince her to try this combination. When we conducted trials much later, we discovered that the combination resulted in reducing the Paclitaxel dosage by 300 times."

Another goal of the research was to ensure targeted delivery of the drug to only the cancer cells, so that healthy cells were not destroyed along with the cancer cells. Other researchers in the area have attempted several ways to achieve this, including engineering the delivery nanoparticle according to the shape and size of the blood vessel that delivers blood to the cancerous cells. Nitin's approach was very different.

"It has been studied that the pH of cancer cells is 5-6, unlike that of healthy cells, which is around 7.4. Also, certain enzymes are found only in cancer cells. We used this information to design our drug delivery mechanism such that it released the drug only when the enzyme and pH conditions are met, ensuring that the drug is delivered only to the cancer cells. As a result, lower dosage of the drug is required to treat the cancer (thus reducing treatment costs) and the debilitating effects of chemotherapy are avoided."

The next challenge was to incorporate controlled drug release. It was very important that the two drugs not be released simultaneously, but one after another, with a time difference of a few hours between them. The nanoparticle had to be specifically designed to ensure this. "Engineering the nanoparticle such that it could deliver all the desired results took us about two years," shares Nitin.

Cancer is one of the leading causes of death worldwide, accounting for about 8 million deaths each year. Lung cancer causes the highest number of cancer-related deaths. Currently, India is home to 3 million cancer patients. There is an unusually high incidence of lung cancer among women in rural India, because the use of wooden and coal-based *chulhas* (stoves) for cooking leads to poor indoor air quality. In other demographics, high exposure to anti-fungal/pest control fumigants and high rate of smoking tobacco are primary reasons.

"This technology can make lung cancer treatment as simple as inhaling asthma medicine. In case of lung cancer, aerosols can be used to inhale drug-containing nanoparticles, which reach the lungs and specifically attack the lung cancer cells. For all other cancer types, these nanoparticles can be injected intravenously and would have the same selectivity and efficacy."

In 2011, Nitin and his guide filed a product patent for the engineered lipid nanoparticles and a process patent for the targeted drug delivery. The process of filing the patent was supported by IIT.

Though the technology would be a big boon to lung cancer patients, the treatment cost is difficult to estimate with full accuracy as yet. The validation cycle for pharmaceutical products is long and several approvals are required before they can be commercialized.

"The costs can be accurately estimated only when the drug is ready to hit the market. However, it should be much cheaper than the best cancer treatment available today."

Nitin was awarded at the International Conference on Nano Science and Technology (ICONSAT), Mumbai in 2010 for his research. This was followed by an award by the Department of Biotechnology, Government of India. In July 2011, with financial support from IIT, Nitin presented his research at the Gordon Research Conference, Maine, USA. He also showcased his work at the American Association for Pharmaceutical Sciences, Washington DC in October 2011. Nitin was featured on the 2012 TR35 India list, a list of most innovative Indians prepared by MIT Technology Review.

Nitin is also a trained classical singer and has been learning from an early age. After years of hiatus, he resumed training his vocal chords after getting into IIT.

Nitin is now continuing his research on nanoparticle - based targeted drug delivery as a post-doctoral fellow at the Harvard Medical College, USA and wishes to pursue an academic career.

For the Innovator in You

"For anyone who wishes to be involved in academic research, choosing the right institution and right guide can be a make-or-break decision. You may not have all the facilities at a second-tier university, or you may lose interest if your guide is not enthusiastic and supportive.

Biotechnology is particularly good for academic research in India these days, because the Department of Biotechnology (DBT) provides good financial support for it. In fact, most of my research work was funded through grants from the DST and DBT. So, if your field of research is related to biotechnology, you can definitely benefit from one of DBT's several schemes."

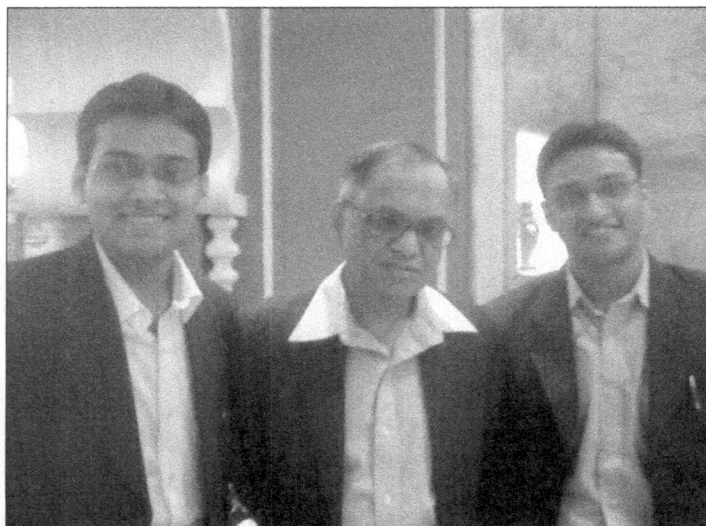

Aniruddha Sharma (left) and Prateek Bumb (right) with
N R Narayanamurthy (center)

CO$_2$ Removal Technology

Prateek grew up in a typical, close-knit Marwari joint family in Jaipur, Rajasthan. Heavily influenced by his brother, Prateek chose to study Commerce in Class XI, in order to follow in his brother's footsteps and become a chartered accountant. As fate would have it, he was forced to move to Kota when his father moved his business interests there.

Kota was a small, sleepy town in Rajasthan, known for its fine-grained limestone, until Mr VK Bansal, an engineer who had to quit his job due to a physical disability, decided to turn it into the mecca for IIT-JEE preparation. He set up Bansal Classes, often referred to as "the factory for IITians". Today, every street in Kota boasts of a coaching institute and thousands of students from across the country flock here to prepare for the tough engineering and medical entrance exams.

"I came to know about IIT only after landing in Kota and decided to give it a shot. I switched to the science stream at my new school in Kota and joined the prestigious Bansal Classes. A few years of hard work later, I found my name on the IIT-JEE merit list and decided to pursue a five-year, dual-degree program in Chemical Engineering at IIT Kharagpur.

The grooming at IIT would perhaps be the single most important reason for my eventual success. I got to learn so much from every person I met there. I learned to work in a team and the environment there pushed me to continuously do better than what I thought I was capable of. My attitude toward learning new things and facing challenges became even more aggressive."

After completing his third year of engineering, Prateek secured a summer internship at University of Perugia, Italy, where he worked on carbon-removal systems for the first time.

Like everything else before that, he excelled at it, and in the process, realized that carbon-removal technologies had several practical applications, especially due to the increased focus of governments around the world on "clean" (more environment-friendly) technologies.

"After returning to IIT, I discussed my work with some friends, including Aniruddha Sharma, who too had worked on a very challenging project during his summer internship at University of Bern, Switzerland."

Interestingly, both Aniruddha and Prateek had prepared for the IIT-JEE in Kota, but didn't know each other until they found themselves in the same classroom at IIT.

The two immediately realized the huge market potential for carbon-removal technology and decided to work together to perfect it and validate the results (that is, ascertain how effective it was in removing carbon from effluents in practice).

"It struck us that so many foreign universities were already working on it, and here in India, we had hardly heard anything about it. We thought if we could develop a technology, there would be a good market for it."

They quickly created a business plan for the "technology to capture CO_2 from industrial flue gases" and sent it as an entry for IDEAS-2008, a business plan competition at IIT Bombay. Their business plan won the third prize.

"It was a shot in the arm. We then decided to take it very seriously and implement the plan.

With our confidence higher than ever, we presented our idea at the Pan-IIT Global Conference in Chennai, the same year. We were awarded the Business Conclave Award jointly by Tata Motors and Tata Steel. To receive that kind of appreciation, from the most illustrious of IIT alumni, was like a dream.

The best part was that the plan earned us more than a trophy, certificate or cash prize. A mentor approached us and entrusted us with some seed capital to validate the results, assuring us that if the results were positive (as good as what had been hypothesized), he would connect us with the right investors."

With this agreement in place, they founded a company, aptly named Carbon Clean Solutions Pvt Ltd (CCS). However, this also brought them face-to-face with their first set of problems.

"We were still at IIT and the labs were not equipped for the kind of experimentation we wanted to undertake. Moreover, any research done or products/processes developed at IIT, using IIT's resources, belong to IIT per the rules. Thus, there could have been difficulties in commercializing it.

There was hardly any technical competency available in the country in this field, so we could not get any mentorship. Also, Kharagpur was too far away from any industrial center; so, it was difficult for us to work with any independent industrial lab while we were still students at IIT.

However, since we were entrusted with the seed fund, we had to produce the results anyhow. So, we started to build all the testing equipment on our own. Therefore, what could have been done in a couple of months with existing testing equipment took us a couple of years."

Meanwhile, Aniruddha got an on-campus placement offer from McKinsey and Company, a leading strategy consulting firm. Prateek, on the other hand, got an offer from INERIS, a public consulting firm in environmental research, based in France. Their parents wanted them to take up the security of a job and the duo had a hard time convincing their respective parents against it. Once their parents relented, they marched on to conquer the next hurdle.

"Once we graduated from IIT in 2010, we started looking for independent labs across the country to tie up with. We first approached National Chemical Laboratories in Pune, but they simply refused to be a part of the project. That was very disappointing, because they are one of the biggest and most sophisticated chemical laboratories in the country and we had pinned our hopes on them.

The search continued for a few more months. Finally, we met with researchers at Institute of Chemical Technology (ICT) in Mumbai, who showed great interest. After formal discussions, we carved out our first Memorandum of Understanding (MoU) with them. Eventually, we established partnerships with IIT Bombay and IIT Delhi as well.

At ICT, we set up a baby pilot plant or test plant. The results from testing revealed that the technology was effective in removing 90% of the carbon dioxide (CO_2) from gaseous effluents. Once the results were established, we filed for product and process patents in 2010."

Prateek explains how the technology works. "The technology involves the use of a proprietary solvent to dissolve the CO_2 from the gaseous effluents in the chimney. This is done via a certain chemical reaction, assisted by a proprietary catalyst at a specified condition. So, the patents cover both – the process and the proprietary chemicals involved.

"Any industry that produces carbon dioxide would need such a system. Currently, our biggest buyers are steel, power, cement, bottling and biodiesel plants. Many countries have strict norms regarding industrial emissions, which force industrial plants to install such a technology. Moreover, the clients can earn carbon credits for the CO_2 emissions prevented. An even bigger reason to install this system is the ability to sell the CO_2 thus captured. The cost of capturing CO_2 using our technology is roughly ₹ 3-3.5 per kg, while it can be sold to manufacturers of industrial gases and carbonated drinks for almost ₹ 8 per kg.

A coal-based power plant typically generates about 20 tons of CO_2 per day for every MW of power it produces. By selling the CO_2 alone, an average-sized plant can recover the cost of the system within three to four years."

Prateek adds that they are much ahead of the competition. "Only four or five companies in the world have competence in this domain. Our technology requires 30% less operating expense (OPEX, that is, the running cost) and 40% less capital expense (CAPEX, that is, installation cost) as compared to others. Thus, it is more cost-effective."

According to the International Energy Agency, the global carbon capture and storage market is worth $27 billion and is expected to grow to $229 billion in two decades. The size of the industry in India is about $2 billion and can be expected to grow to $30 billion over the same period.

Just four years out of IIT, Prateek and Aniruddha have clients in Australia and the UK and are looking to expand into North America and mainland Europe as well. They have received a Technopreneur Promotion Program (TePP) grant from the Ministry of Science and Technology, Government of India and also a £20 million grant from the Department of Climate, Government of UK.

Both Prateek and Aniruddha were a part of the 20-member Indian Youth Delegation to the COP15 conference in Copenhagen, Denmark in 2009. At COP15, they analyzed the environmental impact of the policy decisions highlighted in India's 11th five-year plan and submitted recommendation papers to the United Nations Framework Convention on Climate Change.

CCS' annual revenue has crossed the $1 million mark and the company was recently featured in the coveted *Forbes* magazine. Prateek and Aniruddha are now looking forward to opening an office in the US soon. They expect to attract clients from a variety of industries there for their customized carbon-removal systems, which are touted to be better than those offered by chemical giants such as Dow Chemicals and BASF. To survive in the competitive US market, they plan to expand their R&D capabilities further and diversify into other clean technologies as well.

All at the age of 27.

For the Innovator in You

"Do not compromise on IPR protection. Your technology is the core of the business. So, you should not look for cheaper alternatives while selecting patent lawyers. Also, do not wait too long before you apply for a patent. Get an idea patent as soon as you figure out the commercial potential of the technology you are trying to create.

Finding a good patent lawyer in India is very difficult; get your papers drafted by an American patent lawyer and then take the help of an Indian patent lawyer to file for the Indian patent. Do get a US patent, as it is the biggest market for nearly all technology products, and there are many who can copy your products there if you do not have good IPR protection. Also, the US patent serves as a gold standard for the novelty of a technology and lends it credibility with people around the globe.

It helps if you have a few other people working together on the project with you, rather than doing it alone, as you can benefit from each other's competence and divide responsibilities accordingly.

Lastly, I feel that we did not have a very good idea about the financial aspect of the business, and thus, ended up losing a greater share of our business to the investors than we should have. Thus, I strongly recommend doing proper market research to value your business. If you find it too difficult or confusing, try taking the help of your friends who may have expertise in it or approach consultants specializing in market research.

Investors are astute negotiators and your confidence is the key to getting the right deal. You should try to get only those investors on-board who have the kind of contacts that you require-these contacts are as important as the money, if not more."

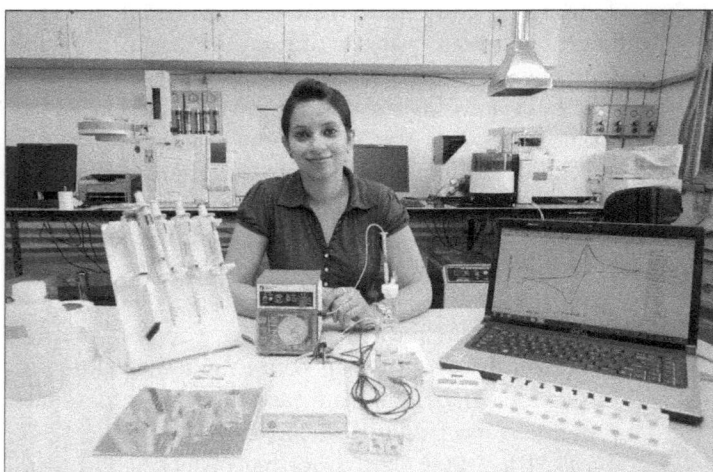

Priyanka Sharma

Ultra Low-Cost Immuno-sensor Biochip for Detecting Environmental Pollutants

Born to an engineer father and a homemaker mother, Priyanka was brought up in the HMT Colony near Chandigarh. Being the only child, she was a pampered kid and being a girl, her parents always wanted her to take up an easy job. Therefore, after completing her MSc degree, she joined a government college in Chandigarh as a lecturer and worked there for three years.

Though she enjoyed teaching, she developed a greater passion for research and decided to make a career in that area. She enrolled for a PhD program at Panjab University, but the lack of funds for research pushed her to explore more opportunities. So, she applied to the University Grants Commission's (UGC) Junior Research Fellowships.

Through a very competitive process, she was selected to work at the Council of Scientific and Industrial Research's (CSIR) Institute of Microbial Technology.

"The environment at CSIR is great for research – well-equipped laboratories, well-defined goals, adequate funding, and above all, very supportive and experienced researchers."

Priyanka's educational background was environment sciences, and that was her area of interest in research too. In her travels to rural Punjab from Chandigarh, she had often seen farmers work with pesticides, bare hands and barefooted, using no protective covering. "These are extremely dangerous compounds. Even when we handle them in the laboratory, we wear protective gloves and robes," she explains.

She delves into little-known aspects of pesticide usage in India. "In our country, there are norms regarding phasing out pesticides, but there are no government regulations on monitoring their use and impact.

Therefore, a pesticide would be legally available only for about 10 years after its first introduction (as pests become resistant to it during this period). The companies would then introduce a new pesticide. Nobody would bother about the negative impact of the last pesticide, its concentration in water, soil or living beings, or how it should be handled to avoid human or environmental disaster. Thus, those who profit from the pesticide trade have no liability toward its harmful effects."

This prompted Priyanka to work on detecting pesticide levels in the soil. "I joined research under Dr C Raman Suri, who had several years of research experience in biosensors and diagnostics. I decided to work on biosensors that can detect pesticide levels in soil and water."

As Priyanka's BSc and MSc degrees were in Environmental Science, she did not know about the biological sciences. It was quite intimidating for her to work with some of the best researchers in the field without adequate knowledge. Therefore, she had to work much harder in the first year to bridge the knowledge gap.

"Thanks to my guide, I could learn much faster than I thought, and by the end of the year, there was already good progress on the project."

A European Union directive sets the maximum permissible limit for any individual pesticide in groundwater at 0.1ng/ml. At this low concentration, detection is quite difficult. Currently, various analytical techniques like gas chromatography (GC), high-pressure liquid chromatography (HPLC), capillary electrophoresis (CE) and mass spectrometry (MS) are used for this purpose. All these methods are complex and time-consuming and require costly, bulky instrumentation. Moreover, preparing samples for these techniques is tedious and requires skilled personnel. For all these reasons, these techniques are unsuitable for field studies and *in situ* monitoring of samples.

Despite the need for an inexpensive, portable device that enables quick determination of pesticide levels for human health and agricultural management programs, little had been done on this front, prior to Priyanka's work.

Priyanka explains her research methodology. "We tagged the pesticide (a popular phenyl-urea herbicide called Diuron, used worldwide with cotton crops) with a protein molecule and injected it into rabbits and chicken, in order to generate antibodies against it. The animals were injected three more times, with a gap of 21 days between two doses (technically referred to as 'three boosters after the first immunization'). The antibodies formed were then extracted from the rabbit's blood and the chicken's egg yolk.

The antibodies were then characterized using the ELISA (Enzyme Linked Immunosorbent Assay, used to detect the presence of a substance in a liquid sample) technique. Characterization refers to whether the antibodies actually respond to the antigen (the external molecule that the antibody is supposed to act against) and to see how specific they are (whether they bind only to the antigen selectively or to a wide range of compounds). Characterization helps to ascertain whether the antibody will be able to associate with the antigen, even when the concentration of the antigen is low, or when there are several other potential molecules (impurities in the water sample) that can potentially compete with the antigen to react with the antibody.

We used the pesticide and the pesticide-protein conjugate for characterization. The pesticide molecule is very small. Generally, when it enters the animal body, the response against it is invoked when it gets tagged with a much bigger protein molecule. Thus, the antibodies generated inside the animal body in response to the injected pesticide are actually produced for action against the pesticide–protein conjugate. Thus, measuring the response of the antibody to the pesticide molecule, in the presence of the pesticide–protein molecule, gave us an idea of how specific the reaction of the antibody would be toward this pesticide, when the pesticide is in small quantities and there are several other contaminants that may interfere with this reaction.

Once the antibodies that had an affinity for the pesticide molecule were identified, the next thing was to fabricate a sensor that was sensitive enough to measure this reaction, portable enough to be carried to the site and cheap enough to ensure that testing the environment for pesticides would be affordable. That's where we innovated.

In order to measure the extent of the reaction between the antigen and the antibody, we decided to convert the chemical reaction output into an electrical signal that could be measured. However, measuring such a small current requires very sensitive electrodes. This required us to use gold for the electrode material, as it has a very high electrochemical sensitivity. Yet, our goal was to make the biosensor as cheap as possible.

We took scrap plastic (rather than a more expensive material), cut it into small pieces and sputtered it with bulk gold. We then used laser ablation (laser-assisted cutting) to demarcate the electrode areas. However, when we did the experiments, we realized that coating bulk gold did not give us the high sensitivity that was required.

So, we experimented with nano-gold instead. The sensor surface was modified by using electro-deposition of a film of Prussian blue embedded gold nanoparticles (PB-GNP). It was quite challenging, but it enhanced electron transfer in the vicinity of the gold electrode, increasing the sensitivity of the assay.

While the sensitivity increased manifold, the cost was also reduced. In addition, the bio-compatibility increased. The antibodies could now sit on the surface of the gold with much more stability."

Priyanka claims that their biosensor is much more cost-effective than existing biosensors. "You will be surprised to know that while existing biosensors cost $100-$600, our biosensor can be made for only ₹ 5."

The biosensor is also very effective for its purpose. "We ran tests with water samples collected from nearby water-bodies, using the fabricated bio-chip and isolated antibodies. Even trace amounts of the pesticide were detected."

The disposable plastic biochip is highly versatile and can be used for any immuno-sensor application, where high sensitivity and low cost are prime concerns. Thus, it can be used for clinical diagnosis, in addition to detecting a variety of environmental pollutants. Low-cost diagnosis is very important in developing countries like India and there is huge market potential for such biosensors.

"My first research paper was published in 2009, in *Biosensors and Bioelectronics*, an Elsevier journal. My parents were overjoyed. My father even took a print of it and tried to understand it.

In the later half of the same year, two more research papers were published and I became a star in my research group within a short period of time. Today, I have 13 publications, in nearly all the reputed journals, including *Nature*.

We applied for the Indian patent in January 2010, and it has already been published. CSIR is now scrutinizing proposals to commercialize the technology."

In 2011, Priyanka bagged the India Innovation Initiative (i3) Award by Agilent Technologies, in association with Confederation of Indian Industries (CII) and DST.

At the age of 28, she was the only woman on MIT Technology Review's list of top Indian Innovators for the year 2012. She also received the DST Lockheed Martin Gold Medal for 2012.

She shares an interesting anecdote related to this medal. The ₹ 1 lakh cash prize that comes with the medal was given in the form of a large check. "I was returning from the event on Shatabadi Express and was holding the fake check. Everybody thought I was a sportsperson. People kept asking me about it. When I told them that I was a scientist, they could not believe it. I guess they were a little disappointed.

My parents received me at the station with a big *band–baaja* group. There were so many onlookers; it was hilarious.

Soon after, the MIT Technology Review's list of top 35 innovators was declared and people from the media flocked to my house. There were interviews, photography sessions and what not. I had never received that kind of attention before. They made me feel like a celebrity."

In 2012, INKTalks, a global organization that hosts some of the greatest thinkers to speak about their experiences, invited Priyanka to Pune to talk about her work and its future applications.

"Apart from the recognition, my research work has brought me a lot of satisfaction and an opportunity to travel the world.

In 2010, I went to Northwestern University in the US as a visiting research scholar. It was an amazing experience. Research work abroad is very different from that in India – it is much more application-oriented and interdisciplinary. Researchers there tend to think much more creatively and are more networked. The experience in the US completely transformed my approach to my work. The skills I learned there made me more effective in research."

Priyanka plans to join a post-doctoral program in India that focuses on interdisciplinary research and allows collaboration with laboratories abroad.

"I plan to further improve the biochip by enabling it to be coupled with micro-fluidic systems to enable automatic preparation of samples to be used with the biochip. This would help in situations where a large number of samples need to be tested, or those being tested have very low pesticide concentration. This would enable screening of several disease markers and environmental pollutants with a very small volume of the sample, which is otherwise difficult."

For the Innovator in You

"The patenting process was easy for me, as every CSIR institution has a patent cell to assist CSIR scientists. Moreover, my guide had extensive experience with patents. However, it can be an intimidating experience, especially for those who have no institutional support.

I suggest doing an online course on intellectual property right protection, offered by World Intellectual Property Organization (WIPO). I also did a WIPO Academy course which allowed me to understand the nitty-gritty of getting a patent. In association with academic institutions across the world, WIPO has several courses on patent laws, filing and the examination process. The courses can be done online and a certificate is awarded on successful completion. Some basic courses are available for free.

In general, any innovator faces a lot of hurdles. When things get really bad, remember that most people give up when they are just about to be successful; do not be one of them. Do not accept defeat before the battle is over. Or, as a popular saying goes, 'Give hope half a chance and despair will not win'."

Sachidanand Swami

Interactive Touch Surfaces

If touch phones and touch tablets were not exciting enough, think about touch tables – interactive, large, touch user interface devices, enabling multiple users to engage with each other via a common interface. Imagine playing virtual air hockey in a mall on a touch table, or a boardroom corporate discussion via a touch table rather than a whiteboard. All this and more might soon become reality, thanks to the accomplishments of Sachidanand Swami.

Hailing from a small city in Uttar Pradesh, Sachidanand made it to IIT Delhi, without any coaching. Preparing for one of the most competitive exams in the world and doing better than the peer group, that too without any formal guidance, calls for a lot of courage and self-confidence. There is definitely no dearth of these qualities in Sachidanand.

"Since the days of my early schooling, I dreamt of doing something big and different in the technology space. IIT seemed to be the perfect place to do that. However, adapting to life at IIT wasn't all that easy. There were immensely bright people all around, many from big cities, prominent schools or famous coaching institutes. It created immense pressure, which led me to neglect academics altogether. I had very poor grades at IIT. Good academic standing sometimes helps you gain credibility with new people – good grades portray you as a sincere person to someone who may have no other parameter to judge you. I feel all the other things that I did could have been easily managed without ignoring academics."

Despite an average academic performance, Sachidanand managed to get a job with AT Kearney, a leading strategy consulting firm. However, it was not the job he was looking for.

"I was enrolled in a five-year Mathematics and Computing degree. In my fourth year, I got involved with touch devices via projects underway at IIT Delhi. The technology sparked instant interest in me. I could see its long-term potential and wanted to continue working on it. Technology has always been my first love and it seemed far more exciting than a consulting job. So, I became an associate researcher at IIT Delhi after graduating and started working full-time on the touch user interface.

After a few months, I received an offer from the Technical University of Denmark (DTU) for a research position. It was a tough choice. Going to DTU meant I would have to stop the research work on touch devices, which I did not want to do; yet, this was an opportunity I did not want to miss. Eventually, I decided to take up the offer and continue my research on the side while in Denmark.

At DTU, I worked on a graphical user interface for city traffic simulation, which relates to programming traffic signals and other elements of the system, in order to ensure smooth flow of traffic, especially during peak hours.

The Danish stint helped me understand the European market better and also imbibe the positives from the research culture in Europe.

After coming back to India, I continued my work on touch devices with renewed vigor and spent the next 15 months perfecting the user experience to international standards."

With help from the Industrial Design Center at IIT Delhi, Sachidanand made a 103-inch tall interactive wall, which could be put to multiple uses, such as gaming, interactive learning or information dissemination. "Much like what you see in Arnold Schwarzenegger's *The 6th Day* or Tom Cruise's

Minority Report, this was an intelligent wall that could interact with the user via touch interface. We put the wall up in the IIT campus for users to interact with and the response was amazing. That's when I decided that it was time to create a company around this product.

After walls, I started focusing on interactive touch tables, because they are more suited to corporate discussions and have more applications and user engagement than a wall."

Sachidanand applied for the Government of India's TePP grant, via FITT (Forum for Innovation and Technology Transfer) at IIT and started work under the guidance of Prof Hanmandlu of the Electrical Engineering Department at IIT Delhi. He also took interns from other engineering colleges who were keen to learn and ready to commit a year.

"Developing software applications for the hardware was the most time-consuming part. We are still working on expanding our software offerings. The touch table in itself is more like a big tablet. The surface area enables a greater number of people to use it simultaneously; however, the key constituent for a great user experience are the applications that can be run on this hardware. Because this product is not aimed at individuals but at businesses, there is a greater need for customization of software applications for the target business. So, for example, a real estate company may ask us to deploy an interactive wall with software that enables users to learn more about their projects at the touch of a finger, provide further details about a property that the user chooses to touch and give a virtual tour of the flat that the user wishes to see, letting him rotate the view or move back and forth, or even letting him customize the home and calculate the price of the flat after customization.

We have so far applied for five patents in all, both for hardware and software. We are currently working on developing gaming applications for the entertainment industry, various business application suites to enable collaboration at work and simulation software for training purposes."

Touch tables form a niche segment in the technology space and are dominated by MNCs like Microsoft and Perceptive Pixel. However, Sachidanand remains unfazed.

"These companies have their own proprietary technology. So, Microsoft's product is different from Perceptive's and so is ours. Though we essentially compete in the same market, our edge is in our costing. Currently, Microsoft Surface SUR-40 costs around ₹ 5 lakh. We would be able to sell our touch tables at about half that cost. Moreover, the battle will be about who is able to develop better applications – so, if we have better software offerings for the education industry, then schools and colleges will have a reason to choose us over Microsoft. Therefore, software development is our current focus, along with greater localization of content."

Sachidanand finally incorporated his company, Invoxel Technologies, in April 2011. He explains, "Invoxel is short for 'Interactive Voxel'. Voxel is the name for a 3D pixel. So, Invoxel would imply an interactive 3D pixel."

Sachidanand talks about his future plans. "In future, we plan to make gesture-based devices, so a user can interact with an interface by just waving their hands in the air or through body movements. We also plan to develop surfaces which have 3D display."

The current focus of the company is the auto industry. They also participated in Auto Expo in 2013. "We count Hero Motors among our clients. We also worked with Audi during the launch of its SUV Q3 in India. The next industry we would target is telecommunications, for which we are in talks with Nokia. Apart from building clients in India, we are also negotiating a few contracts with clients in Europe."

The next goal for the young venture is to secure venture capital funding.

"Initially, my parents helped with the funds. Later, the grants that I secured saw us through. I did not know anything about incorporating or running a company, but some of my friends, who are chartered accountants, came to the rescue. While filing patents too, I depended largely on my friends who had worked at MNCs specializing in providing services related to intellectual property rights. Through most of the development phase, we had very few employees. Now that the products are ready and we have potential clients, we need to secure some external funding in order to scale up."

The Indus Entrepreneurs (TiE), a global non-profit dedicated to nurturing entrepreneurship, has conferred an award on Invoxel for its technology. Faced with competitors like Microsoft, there is definitely a tough battle ahead for Invoxel, but the confidence that this bespectacled 28-year-old possesses is worth appreciating.

"In 1975, Microsoft was a small and unknown start-up, much like ours. In fact, they took five years to develop the first MS-DOS, which they released in 1980. Nobody knew what the future of computers or of Microsoft would be, but the rest, as they say, is history."

This statement is a perfect example of the iconoclastic exuberance the current generation of young Indians displays – a spirit which is so essential for any kind of change, whether technological or otherwise.

For the Innovator in You

"I seriously suggest consulting your knowledgeable friends for advice in matters that you cannot handle yourself. Their opinion would be more trustworthy, as compared to somebody who might benefit professionally from advising you on a course of action. The right friends can be extremely valuable and can take you a long way.

I also suggest that if you are sure about starting a company to sell a product that you developed, then incorporate it as soon as possible. The older the company, the greater is the credibility. In fact, banks usually do not provide loans to firms less than two years old.

Always believe in yourself and your ideas. Remember that they are worth only as much as you believe they are. Do not waste time pondering about obstacles and outcomes. Be courageous to put your thoughts to test in reality. Success will be within your reach only when you start reaching out for it.

Have short-term goals. That will help you keep the focus and drive away desperation. Celebrate every small success. Do not let the pressure of long-term goals hold you back from enjoying the process of getting there."

Sriram Kannan

Location Tracking without GPS

Sriram was born and brought up in Chennai in a Tamil Brahmin family. His father, an engineer by profession, had strong literary interests. Thus, Sriram grew up in a very scholarly environment. After completing his BSc degree in Physics at Madras University, Sriram moved to Bengaluru for a four-year integrated master's degree in Computer Science at the Indian Institute of Science (IISc).

The four years at IISc were full of excitement, as he interacted with some of the brightest people in the country and was introduced to a very enriching academic culture. He also excelled at sports and became the captain of the cricket team at IISc.

After completing his master's degree in 2000, he was hired as a software developer by Texas Instruments (TI) via the campus interview process. His task was to develop software for mobile chipset security.

After five years with TI, an opportunity came up in the R&D center in Japan and he was sent to Tokyo as he knew Japanese. (His father runs a Japanese language institute in Chennai.) In Japan, he worked on hardware design for Open Multimedia Applications Platform (OMAP), a system on chips (SoCs) for mobile multimedia applications, which eventually became quite successful.

The experience in Japan proved to be a turning point.

"OMAP, at that time, was an evolving technology, and as can be guessed, Japan was way ahead. I worked on customized solutions for clients, and for the first time, I was exposed to the process behind conceptualizing and designing a product. I also learned about marketing and product positioning. In contrast, when I used to work in software development, all I got to know was the release date. Sometimes, I did not even know the scope or impact of my work."

After two years in Japan, TI had to scale down its OMAP operations, because it faced stiff competition from local players and the government regulations favored domestic companies (TI is an American company). However, the competence TI had already developed in OMAP was useful for its operations worldwide. Thus, TI offered Sriram the option of setting up an independent consulting practice of his own and ensured him global TI clients.

"I never planned to start a company and knew very little about it. However, this choice was made for me by someone else. I could not continue working at TI, Japan; if I wanted to continue working on the same technology, this was the only route available to me. It was like a golden parachute (an agreement between a company and an employee, specifying that the employee will receive certain benefits if employment is terminated, usually due to change in control).

I took up the challenge and moved back to Bengaluru in 2007."

Sriram named his consulting firm Nivaata, which means "infinite armor" in Sanskrit. Proving to be true to its name, the firm did an infinite amount of work on a variety of mobile technologies over the next two years.

"One of the most memorable experiences was working with i2i Telesource, a company that focuses on integrated solutions in the wireless domain and offers content management services for mobile advertisements, mobile entertainment and mobile commerce. We worked with them to develop telemedicine applications, especially tele-ophthalmology. In short, it means technology that can help people consult a virtual doctor by using their phone. It was during this time that I came across the idea of using cellphone towers for location tracking.

In those days, my father used to travel every fortnight from Chennai to Bengaluru to meet me. I used to pick him up at Whitefield station. The train usually reached the station around 3 AM, but given the nature of the Indian rail system, nothing could be said with certainty. The train would abruptly halt for long periods at stations or crossings. So, if my father set an alarm, he may wake up too early, in case the train was late. If he took the usual delay into account (which, in any case, was difficult to predict), he may miss the station if the train had not been delayed en route. As a result of this anxiety, he stayed awake all night, so that he could call me up in time for me to reach the station to pick him up.

I thought that for someone who is supposedly solving problems for several big mobile companies, why couldn't I solve my own problem? It occurred to me that if I could set up a piece of software on my father's phone that would let me track his position and also automatically message me when he reached a certain place, our problem would be solved. Neither of us would need to be up all night. I could then wake up a little before 2 AM, check his current position and prepare accordingly. If he was on time, I would proceed to the station. If not, then I could simply go back to bed and wait for the wake-up SMS. My father could also sleep peacefully, as I would be able to call him to wake him up when I left for the station. He would not need to be awake to see where the train had reached.

I had a Nokia E72 phone that ran on the Symbian operating system (OS). So, I wrote the code for a piece of software and installed it on my phone. I then took a trip from Bengaluru to Chennai. Every time I reached a station,

I prompted the software to save its name and the location (based on the nearby cellular towers).

I then installed the same piece of software on my father's Symbian phone, and now, my father's cellphone immediately sent me a message as soon as it reached a certain station. Moreover, the software let me monitor the current location of my dad's cellphone via my cellphone and the server installed at my home."

So far, the project was only for personal use and Sriram had not thought about its commercial potential. However, he soon realized that several people were facing a lot of problems with GPS. "GPS drains the battery very quickly, because it consumes a lot of power. Moreover, not all phones are GPS-enabled, and even if they are, reliable GPS coverage may not be available at all places. Attempts to achieve non-GPS based tracking have been made across the world, with differing technologies, goals and degrees of success."

In late 2008, the Android OS was introduced and became a success. The smartphone market started to grow rapidly.

"The introduction of Android seemed like a very good opportunity. Smartphones were now much more capable and affordable. In 2009, I stopped doing consulting work, in order to focus on developing an improved smartphone application for cell towers-based tracking.

Initially, it was difficult to say no to the consulting income. However, it was clear that if I wanted to make a fine product, I had to devote all my time and energy to it. I was confident that there was a real need for it, and thus, was fully committed to taking the product to the market and not giving up easily."

Sriram hired four people, and several revisions later, the final application was ready by mid-2010.

"When you switch on the application installed on your phone, it connects your phone to a cloud server, which can then communicate with your phone. An authorized person can log into the cloud-based server and track the current position of the phone at any time. So, it is a "where-are-you", not a "where-am-I" system, because another person can monitor your location. That is why it was named Verayu (a distorted version of "where-are-you").

The system makes use of Path Adaptive Cell Clustering Technology (PACCT), a patented technology for tracking cellphones using cell towers. As opposed to the traditional triangulation-based tracking techniques, PACCT works on a large database of self-learning cell tower transitions to estimate the location and path taken by a mobile phone."

The system estimates your position based on the cell towers in your vicinity that are interacting with your cellphone and your approximate distance from each of them.

"In order to convince customers about the potential of the technology, I made them use it, rather than giving them a PowerPoint presentation. I had a representative go to the customer a day before my meeting with them and tell them how they could use the server to track my position. The next day, I would have them monitor my movement as I was on my way to their office. They would know exactly when to open the door."

Sriram describes the other useful features of Verayu. "The communication between the server and the phone is not continuous. It is only when the person tracking you wants to know your current position and performs a specified action (sends a request via SMS or logs into the user interface of the server via the internet) that the server establishes contact with the phone to know the current location. So, it is an on-demand system." This saves power, which would otherwise have been wasted if the system tracked the phone continuously.

Because there is no user interface on the cellphone, it further reduces power consumption, as the display is not activated.

Also, you could set up a schedule, for instance, to be tracked from 9 AM to 5 PM on weekdays only. Then, you cannot be tracked when you are off work."

The first few customers for Verayu were companies who were interested in tracking their sales force. "They wanted to use the system to effectively monitor the activities of their salespeople. Using the system, the manager could monitor if the salespeople were actually visiting the client location and at what time.

"Moreover, the data analytics built into the software enabled managers to analyze information such as how much time a particular salesperson spent on servicing a client. This allowed him to judge the performance of the salesperson. Many managers discovered that, for the first time, they could monitor which customers were not being served well enough.

Also, the salespeople could no longer claim expenses they did not incur (for instance, they could not eat at a cheaper place and get bills from a more expensive restaurant for reimbursement, for the manager could track them any time and may already know where they had lunch).

Moreover, the manager could send an SMS to any salesperson on the field via the server. So, if a new service request is generated in the system, the manager could track all the salespeople to see who was the nearest, and then send him a message to service this new request as soon as possible.

If the salesperson switches off the cellphone (which he is not supposed to do), that would also be reported into the system. If the battery is running low, the user is automatically notified of this and is asked to charge it.

In fact, you can even take a picture by using the cellphone, but without pressing any button on the cellphone. Since the cellphone's functions have been teleported to the server, the manager can direct the salesperson to position the phone in a certain way (via an SMS) and then push a button on the user interface on the server. The picture would be taken and immediately received by the manager.

You can also geo-tag your comments and photos on social networking sites via the Verayu application, without using GPS.

The application was so popular with the sales teams of several companies that we struck a partnership with RIM (the makers of Blackberry phones) to provide the application bundled with the phones that these companies purchased for their sales staff.

With software that had the ability to track as well as present performance analytics, we positioned ourselves as Mobile Workforce Management solution providers. Unlike the traditional systems, our system required no training and very cheap hardware (only a smartphone which is as cheap as ₹ 4,000 these days), and yet it delivered superior results. Thus, it was a huge hit."

Sriram then started focusing on providing cheap fleet management systems to the cab companies that served BPOs. The software was enhanced for this purpose.

"The software could now automatically SMS a waiting customer about the current cab location and the estimated time of arrival (ETA), as soon as the cab entered a certain radius from the customer location. Since a call-center cab would take the same route daily, the ETA is automatically calculated based on the average time the cab took to cover the same distance over the last few days. Thus, the software keeps learning.

The system can also be programmed to send out text alerts to an employee's family about his/her whereabouts."

This system, too, was a success. Many call centers now demand fleet owners to compulsorily have Verayu installed in their cabs if they want the contract. Fleet owners can also check if their employees are misusing the vehicle. Moreover, the cost of the system is a fraction of what GPS would cost them. Like the sales managers in companies, fleet owners can also send messages to guide the cab driver. The fleet owners just need to pay a fixed monthly amount for every cab they install the system on.

"One of the fleet owners then asked us if we could make a device that was specifically devoted to Verayu. Since tracking using Verayu does not use the cellphone display, such a dedicated device would not need an LCD screen, and thus, would be even more cost-effective."

Sriram decided to work on the suggestion. "We spent a few months designing and fabricating the device, eventually named Verayu Yantra. Yantra stands for **Y**et **An**other **Tra**cker, as it is like any other tracking device as far as the hardware is concerned. It is the Verayu software that makes it different. It is the size of a matchbox and houses the SIM card, battery and chipset. It is four times smaller than a GPS device and costs about ₹ 2,500. It is so battery-efficient that it can run for two weeks on a single charge. It can also be used by public transport providers.

The location tracking using cell towers is not as accurate as GPS, but it is good enough for most practical purposes except navigation (that is, driving or walking directions). We have tied up with several map agencies to use their geographical information content. Since the system is self-learning, it becomes better as more people use it.

We obtained the Indian patent for PACCT in 2010. We have applied for the PCT in order to obtain patents in several other countries."

Sriram foresees a bright future for Verayu. "There are so many applications for such a product, especially in supply chain management. It can interest a lot of players in the FMCG and retail industries.

Verayu can also be used for security and asset monitoring. For example, you can position a Verayu enabled cellphone in your home and can take a picture using the cellphone camera via the interface of the cloud-based server, which can be accessed from anywhere, at any time, whether you are in office or on holiday. Moreover, antique or precious pieces of jewelry and artwork can be protected by using a concealed Verayu Yantra or creating a geo-fencing which would give an alert if a violation occurs."

Sriram speaks about the company's financial position, in the initial days and now. "Initially, I had to bootstrap the company using my savings. At one time, I had to sell my house to support the activities of the company. At that time, I did not know anything about professional investors. Some of my friends supported me financially during tough times. I cannot thank them enough for their trust. The resolve to return their money pushed me to keep going; otherwise, I could have given up.

I gradually learned about professional investors and started pitching to them. We received our first angel investment in April 2010. We have had four rounds of angel investments so far, totaling $250,000. At the time of the first angel investment, we had just 10 customers; we are now acquiring customers at an average of 55 per week.

Just recently, we closed a $10 million VC funding deal. Raising VC funds proved to be very difficult, despite growing sales revenue and a proven business model."

Nivaata has now opened up their platform for other applications. "We are giving away the API for free, so that businesses can create their own applications that use our platform to get location information. This is called Location as a Service (LaaS). We charge them a fixed monthly fee based on every application that gets installed.

"In the future, the service can evolve to an extent where you can get notified when a Verayu user nears your establishment. You can then lure him by offering special deals, etc. The global market for such location-based services is expected to cross $10 billion by 2015. We are well positioned to get a good cut of it for ourselves."

Nivaata is now offering other services as well, like iTransfr™ and sureLock™. iTransfr is a cloud-based contact management suite which keeps a backup of all your contacts and allows you to retrieve them if your cellphone is lost or damaged. sureLock is a lost phone tracker. Nivaata is looking to partner with all major telecom companies to provide tracking services for phones that use their SIM cards.

"So far, it has been a difficult but satisfying journey. We hope to scale greater heights and leave an indelible mark in the technology space. Seeing one's creation in action is a very pleasant experience. We hope our creations help millions around the globe lead a better life."

For the Innovator in You

"An innovator is always biased toward his innovation. It is important to get feedback from others. Ask your friends and family to use the product and then get feedback from other potential users as well, in order to get a more unbiased judgment. Take their feedback seriously and use the criticism constructively to improve the technology further. If your chosen sample of people do not like it, then chances are good that others may not like it too. Thus, you would know what is likely to appeal to the mass market and what is not.

Innovation and entrepreneurship are linked. These days, there is a lot of enthusiasm regarding entrepreneurship, which is a good sign. However, so many young ventures falter because of lack of proper planning and execution. It is good to be entrepreneurial, but remember that you should not start a company just for the sake of starting one. You should be totally aware of the market potential of your idea/product and have a clear strategy and goals. Getting into entrepreneurship without the right mental preparation, a clear roadmap and patience can lead to desperation and failure."

Abhijeet Joshi

Implantable Biosensor for Diabetes Monitoring

Abhijeet was born in Latur, Maharashtra, but was brought up in Ambernath (near Mumbai), where his father worked as a supervisor in an ordinance factory.

Abhijeet had a carefree childhood with little affinity for academics. Most of his time in school was spent playing cricket; he also represented his school in the sport. After he completed Class XII, there ensued a period of confusion, for he did not know what he wanted to do next.

On his father's insistence, he joined a diploma course in Pharmacy at the University of Mumbai. He did not know much about the subject, but joined the program for the sake of doing something. During the diploma, however, he learned a lot and decided to pursue a career in this field. Because opportunities are limited for diploma holders, he decided to follow it up with a degree course.

Thus, Abhijeet joined the B Pharma program at the University of Mumbai. Years went by rapidly and he appeared for the GATE exam in his final year, obtaining a good score.

This enabled Abhijeet to secure admission in the National Institute of Pharmaceutical Education and Research (NIPER), Mohali, which is the first national-level institute set up by the Government of India for pharmaceutical research and education. It is now an Institute of National Importance and employs eminent faculty in the field of pharmacology in India.

"I changed a lot during my years at NIPER, starting with my shy persona. My fellow students at NIPER came from all parts of the country. Interacting with them was quite enriching. My first brush with research was also at NIPER, where I worked on various aspects of drug delivery and testing. My master's thesis was on soluble drugs, and by the time I graduated, I already had a research article published on the subject.

After I completed my master's degree, I received a job offer from Nicholas Piramal. However, my experience at NIPER motivated me to go into more active research. Therefore, I turned down the offer and joined the PhD program at IIT Bombay.

At IIT, I was associated with the Biomedical Engineering Department. It was unlike anything I had done before. I was from a pure pharmaceuticals background and had to learn a lot of things, but my guide always helped a lot."

As part of his PhD, he started working on an implantable biosensor for blood glucose level monitoring. Little did he know that his achievements over the next few years could have a phenomenal impact on the life of millions of diabetes patients across the world.

Diabetes mellitus or simply diabetes is a condition where the beta cells of the pancreas stop producing sufficient level of the hormone, insulin. Insulin is required for the metabolism of glucose in the body. Thus, the glucose level in the bloodstream rises, and if it is not controlled via external medication, it can cause various complications such as permanent damage to the kidneys and eyes.

Globally, about 250 million people are affected by diabetes. Unfortunately, India is the diabetes capital of the world with almost 50 million diabetes patients; moreover, 11 per cent of the urban population and 3 per cent of the rural population above the age of 15 has diabetes.

In order to control the blood glucose levels in diabetes patients, either oral medication or insulin shots are administered. However, the amount of medication needs to be controlled, because excess medication can lead to hypoglycemia – a drop in blood glucose levels way below the healthy level. Because the human brain uses only glucose for energy, low blood glucose levels can cause a person to faint or even die. Therefore, in diabetes patients, the blood sugar level needs to be monitored regularly to ensure that the medication is neither too high nor too low.

Blood glucose levels are usually measured by using external assaying techniques which require pricking the patients and collecting their blood samples. The idea behind Abhijeet's work was to find a way to implant a stable, biodegradable sensor in a patient's subcutaneous tissue, which can then provide the value of his blood glucose level at any time, by using an external, non-invasive probing method.

The work was very challenging on many fronts. "If you put an external substance into the human body, it reacts by producing antibodies against it. This reaction can cause several harmful side-effects. Moreover, the implant should be absolutely sterile and made of a biodegradable material, so that it does not stay in the body forever. Also, the metabolic products that it produces must be non-toxic."

Abhijeet shares the details of his research. "Glucose oxidase is the enzyme that reacts with glucose and breaks it into products that can be detected and measured. We had to design a matrix (a material in which the enzyme could be encapsulated) which is stable (so that it does not disintegrate too fast in the body) and fulfills all the other conditions.

"After a lot of study and trial-and-error, we finally selected a combination of alginic acid, gelatin and albumin. All of these are naturally occurring, stable proteins, and can easily be injected into the subcutaneous tissue. They also degrade over time without producing any toxins or inviting a response from the immune system.

We then added a fluorescent dye to the matrix, which glows when it is subjected to near-infrared radiation. We decided to use a wavelength of almost 600 nanometers (nm) to irradiate the dye. The human skin hardly absorbs radiations of this wavelength, and thus, we could irradiate the matrix in the subcutaneous tissue. The intensity with which the dye glowed upon irradiation depended on the glucose level in the blood. So, the higher the glucose level, the higher the intensity would be. The intensity can then be measured and the associated blood glucose level ascertained by using the already established calibration curve."

Abhijeet explains the working of the biosensor. "The glucose oxidase present in the injected matrix constantly reacts with the blood glucose. If the concentration of blood glucose is high, the concentration of the products of this reaction would be high as well, which would make the dye glow more brightly when irradiated with 600 nm radiation. The process of conversion of the intensity of glow to the blood glucose level reading can be automated via an external device.

So, once the matrix is injected, anybody can monitor the blood glucose level at any time by just directing a light beam from the device, without the need for pricking, and decide the amount of medication accordingly. Once injected, the dye-and-enzyme-containing matrix can last for several days. Thus, it need not be injected too frequently."

He shares the hurdles along the way, technological and otherwise. "The major hurdle was finding a way to prevent the matrix from diffusing into the blood vessel and flowing away with the bloodstream. A lot of effort went into ensuring that this does not happen. After several trials, we put the nanoparticles of the matrix into a microsphere (that is, balls with a diameter of one micron). Nanoparticles can diffuse into the blood, but not micron-sized particles. In order to monitor whether we were successful in preventing the diffusion, we put magnetic nanoparticles on the microspheres and injected them into the subcutaneous tissue of mice. We then subjected the mice to regular MRI scans in order to monitor the position of microspheres. This confirmed that our effort was not in vain.

Next, we had to prove that there were no side-effects. Again, trials were conducted on rats and the results were encouraging. The injected biosensor lasted for a month and did not have any side-effect.

Intellectual Ventures, an IPR-based company (that is, a company that purchases patents and helps in their commercialization), which has a research partnership with IIT-B, helped us with the patent filing process.

When we were nearing the completion of our project, a team from Intellectual Ventures was visiting to review the progress of certain other projects. They came across our work accidentally. They were impressed with what they saw and decided to support it.

There were many hiccups during the development phase. At times, chemicals like high-purity enzymes, which were not available in India, had to be imported and it took longer than anticipated. Sometimes, the work had to be stopped because the funds dried up. However, Intellectual Ventures have been very supportive ever since they joined us. They have a lot of confidence in the commercial viability of the work. So, in the end, our patience and perseverance proved to be the winner."

The scope of his work is not limited to just diabetes monitoring. The same matrix can be used to encapsulate another enzyme called lactic oxidase, which breaks down lactic acid. Lactic acid is produced in muscles as they work and causes them to "tire". Embedding lactic oxidase into the injected matrix would help monitoring the lactic acid levels in muscles (like glucose oxidase does for the glucose level in blood). This information can be used to monitor the fitness levels of athletes.

"So, you can monitor the lactic acid levels after, say, an hour of training; or identify the muscles that are tiring faster and need to be strengthened to ensure improved performance.

Also, in the case of heart patients, their heart muscles are weak and should not be strained. Exercise strains heart muscles, and yet, heart patients should exercise to improve their heart function. However, excess exercising can lead to heart failure. Monitoring the lactic acid levels in the heart muscles can be a life saver for heart patients. The moment they reach levels of lactic acid that may be dangerous, they can stop and take rest."

Abhijeet aims to take his work forward and ensure that the product hits the market soon.

"Currently, we are working to add controlled drug release to the matrix, that is, automated drug release in the right amount at the right time when the biosensor senses the need. This would set diabetes patients absolutely free, with nothing to worry about."

In 2012, Abhijeet was awarded the Dr Gaargi Bishnoi Award for Best PhD Thesis and was also named as a promising young innovator by MIT Technology Review. He has received the Rapid Grant for Young Investigators (RGYI) from the DBT, Government of India, to further his research as a post-doctoral fellow at IIT Bombay. DBT has also awarded him the Innovative Young Biotechnologist Award (IYBA). He has presented his work at conferences across the world and received a lot of appreciation. It is really worth appreciating his endeavor, which has brought Abhijeet a long way from being a diploma holder in pharmacology to an ace researcher.

For the Innovator in You

"Every experience adds up to make us what we become, so try to get exposure to as many different fields as possible. This will expand your horizons and give you a new perspective, which will enhance your creative ability.

Do not be fearful of failure. Take your chances; be patient during the tough times and enjoy the process without feeling pressured about achieving success."

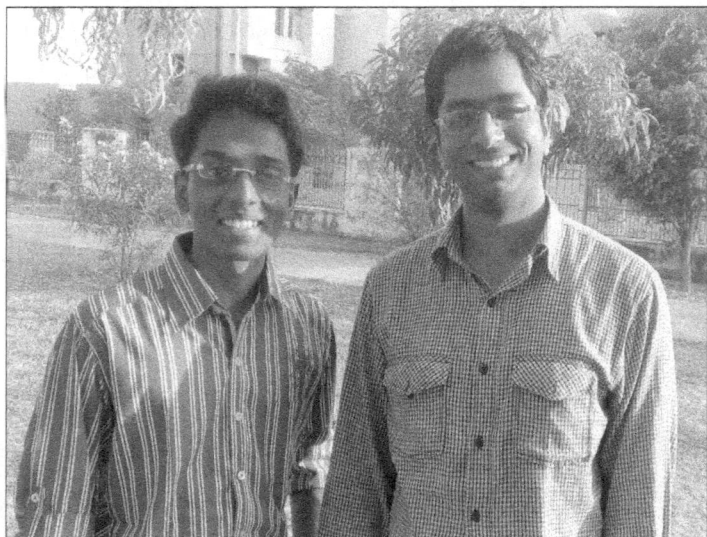

Ganesh (left) and Pragyanandesh (right)

VORWIS

Imagine being able to wear your personal computer on your eyes and carry it everywhere with you, interact with it via gestures (and not a keypad or mouse), with everything displayed in 3D, merging the real and virtual worlds.

This and much more, is what the duo of Ganesh and Pragyanandesh aim to achieve.

Ganesh comes from Vizag, Andhra Pradesh while Pragyanandesh (referred to as Pragyan) hails from Varanasi, Uttar Pradesh. Their journey to IIT has been as interesting as their travails after getting into the Institute.

Ganesh was an average student until Class IX, but he managed to get a good score in the Class X Board exams. His performance, along with a little luck, landed him a place in the topmost batch of the most prestigious IIT-JEE coaching institute in Vizag. There, he came into contact with some of the brightest people he had ever met and their company had a magical impact on him. By the end of the two-year coaching period, he was a "topper among the toppers" and was even sent by his coaching institute to Hyderabad for a 24-hour intensive crash course, just before the IIT entrance exam. Armed with immaculate preparation, he aced the IIT-JEE in 2009 with an All India rank of 121.

If Pragyan is to be believed, his academic performance in school was worse. He almost failed Class X. In Class XI, however, he developed some interest in academics for the first time, as he found the curriculum much more practical than in any of the previous classes. At that time, he was enrolled in a school in Bihar because his father, a Principal at Navodaya Vidyalaya, was posted there.

Pragyan became very inquisitive and started reading beyond his textbooks. His scores improved as well, which further fuelled his interest. Unfortunately, just as he was finally beginning to enjoy his studies, he had an accident on his way to school and fractured his leg. He was bedridden for the next six months and had to drop the year. This was a very frustrating and depressing period for him, but with the kind of determination he possessed, he was able to bounce back and did well in the class XII Board exams.

At that time, he knew little about IIT. Many of his friends were dropping a year to go to Kota and prepare for the IIT-JEE, so he too followed them to Bansal Classes. The preparation helped him develop a problem-solving attitude and made him realize that with hard work, he could achieve any goal he set his eyes on. The grueling work was not wasted, as he ended up with an impressive rank of 550, becoming one of the last few to secure admission into IIT Kanpur's Electrical Engineering Department that year.

Ganesh and Pragyan met at IIT and struggled through the first year together, scoring 6 point GPAs. The academic environment at IIT was very different from what they had expected and they couldn't adjust well. They found the course to be too theoretical, with parts of the curriculum being too outdated to have any practical value in today's world. The "dull and boring lectures" failed to hold their attention.

Thus, they started exploring the plethora of extra-curricular opportunities available at IIT and ventured into the Electronics Club. The opportunity to do more hands-on work at this Club caught their fancy.

With guidance from the club members, Ganesh made a GPS navigation system from scratch, in the summer break right after the first year. Meanwhile, Pragyan worked on several different things.

Pragyan recounts how they collaborated on their first project together. "In our second year, we worked together to make an improved version of the digital diary that could sync with any other device and could be fabricated in just ₹ 600. We presented the digital diary at *Aavishkaar*, the annual technology festival of Motilal Nehru National Institute of Technology, Allahabad. It won us the third prize in the competition. Though it was good for intellectual satisfaction, it didn't make sense to pursue it beyond this point, because digital diaries were out of fashion."

The same year, they developed a GSM-based electric billing system, which could be set up to monitor the power consumption of any device or house from anywhere, in real time.

Ganesh explains how the system worked. "It consisted of two parts. The first was the device that measured the electricity units consumed (like the conventional meter) and transmitted this information to a server via a GSM chipset. The second part consisted of the server and the website. Once the power consumption data is received by the server, it calculates the electricity bill per the billing rate built into it. This information can be viewed at the website in real time. The website can then be used to directly pay the bills. This is especially useful in places where there is a different billing rate for peak and the non-peak hours. So, people can monitor the billing and wisely choose how much to consume during the peak hours (when the rate is high). This is one of the facilities that smart grids provide in some western countries."

They presented this idea at *Kshitij*, IIT Kharagpur's technology festival and received a lot of appreciation. In fact, a professor from IIT Kharagpur approached them with an offer of ₹ 150,000 to commercialize it, but they declined the offer.

"We had seen a senior student do something similar on a commercial scale and fail. We were not too sure if there was a ready market for it as yet," Pragyan explains. "We learned a lot through that project and felt that we would rather use that learning somewhere else, where we can make a marketable product, rather than taking this further and end up like that senior.

It was around this time that we came across Pranav Mistry's work through his TED videos. His technology, popularly known as the SixthSense, is a wearable gestural interface that augments the physical world around us with digital information and lets us use natural hand gestures to interact with that information. It reminded me of the work I had done in my mathematics laboratory project in Class X, where I converted a mathematics textbook from 2D to 3D and found that learning through that textbook became much more enjoyable.

We were deeply inspired by Pranav's work, but we found a few things that could be improved upon. For example, to use Pranav's technology, one needs to wear special color-coded devices on the fingers. Moreover, the camera projects only 2D images. We thought about interaction with 3D objects in the virtual world, like we do in the real world."

Thus, their project, VORWIS stands for Virtual Object in Real World, Interaction and Sharing. That's exactly what the project aims to achieve.

To understand this some more, suppose you are playing a car-racing game on your computer. You see a car on your 2D screen and direct it via the arrow keys and accelerate its speed via the spacebar. Now, imagine a system that can be worn like eyeglasses. When you play the game on this system, it lets you experience a virtual 3D car as if you are sitting in it. You can control the car like you do a real one – by gesturing as if you are holding the steering wheel of this virtual 3D car and pressing the accelerator. Moreover, you can see the competing virtual cars around you as you vroom past them.

"With this idea in mind, we started working on the technology for creating a projection of 3D objects in air," says Ganesh. After a month of work, we realized that we would not be able to do it without Virtual Retina Display, a technology that is still under active research across the world. Meanwhile, we still had to figure out how people would interact with that virtual 3D object."

Virtual Retina Display (VRD) is a technology developed by Human Interface Technology Lab, Washington DC, USA. The technology aims to bring vision to those who have damaged eye lenses but a working retina. When the colored light obtained from the reflection of white light from a particular object is focused by the eye lenses on the retina, certain cone and rod cells in the retina are activated, which help us perceive that object. Using VRD, the same rods and cones are activated via low intensity colored laser beams which can be directly focused on the retina, enabling vision.

Pragyan says that they decided to go ahead with their basic idea. "In January 2011, we decided to apply to the India Intel Embedded Challenge. We did not have much hope, but did it just for the sake of it, because there was no harm in trying. Thus, our first abstract on the 'Technology to interact with virtual 3D objects with gestures' was submitted.

In February, we submitted the final abstract and it was selected. The funny part was that we still had no idea how we would realize what we had hypothesized.

Interpretation of gestures required capturing the gestures via a camera and then developing software codes to identify each gesture and perform the action intended by it. We had no idea which camera we should use to capture the depth of 3D objects or actions. Around the same time, Microsoft came out with the Kinect for Xbox 360. The Kinect sensor captures 3D motion, as it is capable of recording the depth data that normal cameras cannot.

We heard that the Computer Science Department at IIT Kanpur had bought a Kinect and decided to approach a professor at the Department to let us use it. We were not too sure if permission would be granted. However, the professor immediately arranged for all the required permissions when he heard what we intended to do with it.

We were already in May 2011, and were running short on time," Ganesh adds. "But that's what you learn at IIT – working toward tight deadlines. Once we had the Kinect sensor, we started working on the library of software to enable recognition and interpretation of gestures.

Because we wanted to implement direct recognition of gestures without the need for any additional devices or color coding, the algorithm was very complex. Further, we also did not intend to project the graphical interface on a 2D surface, like in Pranav Mistry's work. This added to the complexity.

Anubhav Singla, one of our seniors and a coordinator with the Electronics Club, helped us a lot. He had been part of the Intel Embedded Challenge earlier and gave us useful insights. Finally, in August 2011, we made the final presentation on our work in front of a jury. They were deeply impressed with what we had achieved and adjudged us the winners in the Educational Technology category. Though the competition ended, we continued with our work, using ₹ 50,000 that we won."

Pragyan explains how the technology works. "With our system, you would be able to see the 3D image on special eyeglasses. You would also be able to view the real-world objects around you at the same time through those glasses. Moreover, you can take a real object into the virtual world, if you come within a certain distance of that object and perform a certain action. Say, you want to solve an unsolved Rubik's cube lying in your room. You can go within a certain distance of the Rubik's cube, take a 3D picture of that cube, and then solve it as a virtual 3D object by using your hand gestures, like you would for the real cube. So, you have solved that Rubik's cube without even touching it. It still lies unsolved, at the same place; yet, you have done whatever you intended to do with it.

This is not all. You can interact with real and virtual objects at the same time. For instance, you are having a one-to-one video chat with one of your friends, and his 2D picture is on the screen. Or picture this – another friend enters the room and stands behind your computer screen. You will see only that part of him/her that is not being covered by the computer. On the computer screen, you will see only your chat friend. Now imagine a system that lets you see your chat friend in 3D, as if he is standing right in front of you, like a real person. Now, when another friend enters the room, it appears that there are two persons in the room, rather than just one real person. So, the virtual object merges into the real environment. Thus, this technology blurs the difference between the real and virtual worlds."

Ganesh adds that VORWIS is very different from Google Glasses. "VORWIS would enable us to share what we are seeing live through our eyes, in real time with our friends. It is much like what the Google Glass Project promises, but much better. With Google Glasses, one interacts via buttons placed on the sides of the glasses; while in our case, the interaction is via gestures. Plus, we are not too sure whether Google even plans to have virtual 3D objects. Their offering is based on conventional 2D displays.

Google Glasses were announced in early 2012. We conceptualized our idea in 2010 and have been working independent of any other group, developing our own technology.

The project consists of three parts: Visualization of 3D objects, Interaction with 3D objects and Sharing of 3D objects."

Ganesh and Pragyan share the current status of the project and future plans. "We have completed work on the interaction part and are currently working on the sharing part. Sharing would enable collaboration; for instance, several friends can together solve the Rubik's cube and any change made by any of them would reflect on everybody's screen. Also, the technology can interact with other digital devices such as smartphones. So, you can get 3D map navigation on your glasses by using the 3G internet connection on your phone.

For the visualization part, we need to work with hardware (VRD) vendors like Microvision and that would come next. Meanwhile, we are trying to start with the patenting process.

Our parents do not really understand what we are doing, but they think it must be something really good because it sounds quite hi-tech. They have an idea that we may not apply for campus placements, but they have been quite supportive."

With the path charted out so clearly and so early, these two geniuses are all set to leave an indelible mark on the world of computing.

For the Innovator in You

"We strongly believe in the Law of Attraction – if your desire is strong and you work hard enough to achieve it, then you start attracting the result you wish for.

For those who are still in college, we suggest that if you have a great idea, do not wait. College is probably the best time and place to try out your idea, because there is hardly any pressure from the fear of failure and ample institutional support is available.

If you are smart enough to do something innovative, then you will definitely find a job waiting for you, if you ever need it."

Ahmed Khan, Managing Director, KK Plastic Waste
Management

Road Construction using Plastic Waste

For the generation that grew up learning that plastic waste is an ecological disaster, Ahmed Khan is a pleasant surprise. In an age where governments across the world have failed to find a solution to the plastic waste menace, he seems to have found the perfect answer.

Ahmed Khan was born to a school-teacher father and homemaker mother and grew up in a village in the Mandya district of Karnataka. In the early 1980s, he set up a polybag production unit in Bengaluru, in partnership with his brother, Rasool Khan. Starting with the polybags used in nurseries, the Khan brothers had made KK Plastics a well-known name in the industry by the early 1990s.

In 1995, however, the first set of legislations against the use of plastic came into effect, which was a blow to their business. Retailers started replacing plastic bags with those made from paper. Sales at KK Plastics dipped for the first time in years.

"Municipal corporations around the country have found it extremely difficult to handle plastic waste which threatens soil fertility, the life of stray animals and free flow of sewage through ill-maintained municipality pipelines. Banning plastic polybags seems to be a plausible solution, but unfortunately, it inevitably gets replaced by paper, which isn't ecologically viable either," says Ahmed.

He describes the problems of using paper bags. "Apart from causing large-scale deforestation, making paper pulp consumes as much as 20 liters of water for every kilogram of pulp produced. Moreover, the dioxins produced during the bleaching process have the potential to cause immunological, neurological and developmental ailments. Yet, paper bags fail to match the high strength and light weight of their plastic counterparts; neither do they possess any resistance against pests or water. Thus, they have a very short shelf life as compared to plastic polybags and require more frequent recycling. The waste paper releases methane upon rotting, which is a highly potent greenhouse gas."

Ahmed states that banning plastic polybags is not a solution. "Plastic polybags are just the tip of the iceberg. Plastics form a part of almost everything we use on a daily basis – PET bottles, sachets and so on. Thus, it is almost impossible to get rid of them. Using glass bottles for milk instead of plastic bottles, in addition to being more expensive, would be a big hassle. Recycling these bottles uses a lot of water for cleaning, and if they still remain unclean for some reason, they may pose a health hazard. Also, transporting glass bottles requires special arrangements to prevent breakage, which increases the total volume, and thus, the transportation cost and fuel used, ultimately resulting in higher carbon emissions. In short, given the alternatives, banning plastic polybags does not serve the purpose of protecting the environment as well as it is projected to. A more pragmatic approach is to create systems to handle plastic waste in a better manner.

The policy focus should be on implementing ways to segregate plastic waste at the point of origin, so that it can easily be recycled or put to some other constructive use, rather than ending up in landfills along with all other municipal solid waste."

Ahmed shares what prompted the company to explore plastic waste management. "We realized that being among those who produce plastics, we should own up to the moral responsibility of finding an eco-friendly way of disposing of the plastics. Therefore, we set out on a path to discover meaningful uses for plastic waste."

Though neither of the brothers had a degree in science, they set up a small laboratory within the factory premises and started experimenting with plastic waste. "At first, we tried to make a construction brick from it. Those efforts did not yield results, and soon, we had to abandon the idea.

"It then struck us that plastics and bitumen, both being derivatives of petroleum, may have complementary properties. So, we started mixing bitumen with molten plastic and studying the results.

There were several failed attempts, as bitumen was not easily miscible with molten plastic. However, we did not give up. We had a strong intuition that bitumen, when mixed with plastic, should have better strength when used for laying roads."

Their efforts were finally successful, when they mixed molten plastic at 120°C with bitumen and it yielded a consistent mixture. "We did not know the properties of these substances in great detail. We did not follow a systematic approach or use sophisticated equipment. We just tried whatever we thought could work, and luckily, one of them worked. It was all very simple."

In order to test the strength of the mixture, the company used it to fill potholes on Bengaluru city's roads, filling almost 1,000 potholes in various parts of the city over the course of a year. "The results were very encouraging. The filled potholes survived the rainy season without any sign of damage."

The next step was to adopt the technology on a large scale. "We decided to approach L&T to license our technology to them. However, L&T refused to buy it, saying that they were authorized to use only government-approved materials for road construction; thus, we needed an approval from the government for our technology before they could consider buying it."

"Getting approval from government authorities required getting approvals from the research institutes authorized to test and validate construction material. We approached the Central Road Research Institute, a CSIR institute for road technology, to get our technology evaluated.

Meanwhile, Rasool's son, Amjad, who was studying Civil Engineering at RV College of Engineering, presented the technology to one of his professors. The professor was very impressed and proposed to conduct further research and refinement. He proposed partnering with Bangalore University's Highway Engineering Department for this purpose. We agreed to fund the study; IIT Madras was also involved in the project. Their findings added credibility to our claims that the proposed technology results in longer lasting roads.

Despite the results, obtaining approvals proved to be slow, taking almost three years. However, once we had the required approvals, we confidently approached the Chief Minister of Karnataka, Shri SM Krishna, in 1999.

The CM was very supportive. He wanted to implement the technology across the state for road construction, but the bureaucracy vehemently opposed this, because their interests were aligned with the status quo.

They created all sorts of roadblocks, questioning the technology and even the intention. But the CM prevailed. He directed the BBMP, Bengaluru's municipal corporation, to cooperate with a 30-km pilot project along Raja Rajeshwari Road.

After years of patience and several hiccups, the 30 km stretch was ready in 2002. We waited for a year for the superior strength of the road to be recognized. Despite a heavy monsoon, the road remained as smooth as if it was laid yesterday. The authorities were amazed with the results.

However, the bureaucrats wanted the road to be tested over a few more monsoons, and thus, the clearance was put on hold. Meanwhile, we proceeded with filing the patent for the technology.

Even after three years, the road was as good as new, and the *babus* were finding it increasingly difficult to defer the matter. The technology was finally granted approval for road construction in 2005. Raja Rajeshwari Road is still undamaged, even after 10 years."

Road construction using the technology took off after that, until the next roadblock. "We constructed 530 km of roads across Bengaluru in the next two years, before being bogged down by an unanticipated problem – lack of enough plastic waste. Even though Bengaluru was generating as much as 100 tons of plastic waste per day, we found it difficult to collect enough to keep the construction going."

To deal with this, the company formed another arm called KK Plastic Waste Management to manage the plastic waste collection process. "We offered to buy plastic waste from the rag-pickers at ₹ 6 per kg, which was much higher than the 40-50 paise per kg they used to get. The word spread among the rag-pickers, and soon, they started bringing in as much as 25 tons of plastic waste per day.

Unfortunately in India, unlike in many western countries, there is no practice of separating recyclable waste (plastics, paper and glass/metal) at the point of origin (that is, people disposing of used paper, plastic and glass/metal in separate bins at their homes and offices). Thus, the rag-pickers are forced to collect it, which is unhygienic and inhuman, and still, they get a very poor price for their labor."

KK Plastic Waste Management initiated a plastic collection drive at schools in Bengaluru. They educated children about the harmful effects of plastic waste on the environment and asked them to pass on the message to their parents. Children were encouraged to ask their parents to put

School children being shown the plastic waste collection,
segregation, cleaning and grinding process

the plastic waste in separate bins. The plastic waste collected
at home could be brought to the waste plastic collection center
at the school and the school was paid ₹ 6 per kg for the waste
collected, which could be used toward buying library books
and computers.

Collection centers were also set up in several housing
societies, in cooperation with the respective Resident Welfare
Associations.

"People used to pay to get the waste collected from their
homes, and now, they were getting paid for it. The price
of ₹ 6 per kg served as a good stimulus for people to start
handling their plastic waste themselves."

The collected plastic waste is segregated into different
grades, cleaned, made into a fine powder and then taken to
the construction site. At the site, the powder is mixed into
bitumen in a proprietary ratio at the aforesaid temperature

in hot rollers. The patented mixture, called **KK** Polyblend, is then used to lay roads. Currently, the company charges the municipal corporation ₹ 27 for every kilogram of **KK** Polyblend used.

"The price of road constructed by using **KK** Polyblend turns out to be almost the same as that of the conventional road. However, the life and quality of the road is much higher than the conventional road. If we pay the rag-pickers lesser, we can lower the construction cost, but we would not like to do that."

KK Plastic Waste Management has laid 1,200 km of roads so far, all across Karnataka. They have also received invitations from several other states to present the technology or execute pilot projects.

Because developed countries also face similar concerns in disposing of plastic waste, the US Department of State invited the Khans to make a presentation on their technology at a multinational summit in Malaysia in 2010. The company is currently in talks with a foreign civil contractor for executing joint projects across the world.

In 2008, CNN-IBN honored Ahmed with the Real Hero Award. His efforts toward plastic waste management have also been mentioned in the NCERT Class XII Biology book under the section on Environmental Issues.

He, however, laments the lackluster working of municipal corporations in India.

"Unfortunately, road construction, being the domain of government bodies, is full of red tape. Receiving payments from the government agencies for work performed is a very slow process. It takes between six months and a year to receive payments after completing the project. This blocks working capital. Sometimes, you are even asked to grease palms to get your own hard-earned money."

The Khans are looking for infusion of capital into their company to make an automated plant capable of generating huge volumes of KK Polyblend in a short time, so that they can speed up the road laying process. Each such plant would cost ₹ 3-5 crore.

Ahmed's battle against plastic waste does not end with KK Polyblend. He is also helping a friend develop long-lasting and good-looking furniture from a blend of powdered plastic waste and wooden shavings. The furniture pieces would have as much as 80% of waste plastic and would be termite resistant.

For the Innovator in You

"If your innovation is aimed at the public sector, then you must learn to be patient in order to get your foot in the door. Getting the technology validated by independent laboratories is imperative in such cases. It is good to get the technology tested by several labs, if possible.

Innovation is not a linear process from A to B. One needs to try several possibilities. Failure is a part of the innovation process. Take failure as an opportunity to make a new, more intelligent start."

Team Papyrus Efficiencia: (L to R) Pratik Mahapatra, Anurag Kyal,
Snehasis Patra and Subham Debnath

Environment-Friendly Paper

The first paper-like substance was invented by the Egyptians over 6,000 years ago. It was named papyrus, and is also the root of the English word, paper. Papyrus was made by weaving fibrous plants together and pounding them into a flat sheet.

Later, the Greeks and Romans created a kind of parchment paper by using animal skins. However, paper, as we know it today, came into being in 105 AD, when a eunuch in China, named Cai Lun, mashed mulberry bark, hemp and scraps of cotton with water and dried a layer of the mixture in the sun on a linen cloth.

As the Chinese culture flourished and expanded to the edges of the Asian continent, paper went with it to Korea and Japan, and finally reached Europe in 1009 AD via the port city of Valencia in Spain. In the 13th century, Arab traders introduced paper in India, where it replaced the traditional clay tablets and dried leaves as writing material.

However, the real revolution came about with the invention of the printing press by Johannes Gutenberg in Germany in 1453. The subsequent boom in literacy rates led to a sharp rise in demand for paper for printing books.

Today, almost 300 million tons of paper is used annually across the globe. The global economy is highly dependent on paper. Everything from currency to official documents and from packaging material to books requires paper. Paper accounts for 2.5% of industrial production and 2% of world trade.

The current size of the global paper industry is pegged at almost $350 billion. With a growing population and rapid economic progress in emerging markets, the demand for paper is set to double by 2020, despite measures to introduce electronic documentation. Among other things, the ban on plastic polybags has led to a sharp rise in the use of paper as a substitute material in manufacturing shopping bags.

Paper production is the third most energy-intensive of all industrial manufacturing activities, accounting for 12% of the total energy used in the industrial sector.

Though the sophistication of the paper-making process has increased over the centuries, there has been little change in the raw material used.

As a result, each year, over 4 billion trees are cut to supply raw material for paper. A recent mapping of a change in Earth's forest cover by Google Earth revealed that forest cover is being lost at an alarming rate of 2,100 square kilometers per year. The ecological impact of such large-scale deforestation is immense. Still, the demand for wood pulp exceeds its supply, leading to higher prices of wood pulp, and thus, paper, which also puts financial pressure on the end user.

Moreover, the papermaking process releases a variety of chemical pollutants. According to the US Toxic Release Inventory report published by the US Environmental Protection Agency (EPA), pulp and paper mills are among the worst polluters of air, water and land. The paper and pulp industry is also the fourth largest emitter of greenhouse gases in the manufacturing sector. The WorldWatch Institute offers a similar assessment for the rest of the world. Each year, thousands of tons of highly toxic chemicals such as toluene, methanol, chlorine dioxide, hydrochloric acid and formaldehyde are released into the air and water from papermaking plants around the world. These chemicals are capable of causing respiratory, reproductive and skin diseases.

Paper can be recycled up to seven times. Yet, owing to the usage pattern of paper, only about 40% gets recycled; the rest decays in landfills and produces methane, a greenhouse gas which is 23 times more potent than carbon dioxide.

Among all this bad news, the good news is that some budding technologists seem to be making headway in changing the way paper is made.

A team of biotechnology students from Kalinga Institute of Industrial Technology (KIIT), Bhubaneswar, Odisha – Pratik Mahapatra, Anurag Kyal, Snehasis Patra and Subham Debnath – has found a solution to the paper menace, which kills many birds with one stone.

Anurag takes us back to the summer of 2011, when their exciting journey into the world of innovation started as a small project....

"At the end of our first year of engineering at KIIT, we were looking for summer internships. We applied to various research organizations around the country, but received no response. We were not sure about what would interest us, but still applied wherever we could.

However, our efforts were bearing no fruit. So, we approached one of our teachers, Dr Vishakha Raina, an environmental microbiologist, for help.

Dr Raina said that she could give us a very interesting internship, but was not sure how serious we would be about it.

In order to make sure that we wanted to do some meaningful work and were not looking for mere certificates, she set the condition that she would not give us any certificates for our work. We readily accepted that.

She explained that she was recently approached by the Chilika Development Authority (CDA, the authority responsible for the upkeep of the famous Chilika Lake and surrounding areas) in order to find a solution to a fast-growing

weed that was threatening to destroy the beauty of the tour-
isty lake.

"The alkalinity-resistant weed had occupied 50 square
kilometers of the lake. This not only affected the area available
for boating, but also caused increased sedimentation and
threatened the livelihood of the local fishermen. The weed
consumed most of the oxygen in the water, resulting in death
or migration of fish and other creatures (Chilika Lake has
the largest population of endangered Irrawaddy dolphins in
the world). Thus, the ecological balance and biodiversity of
the lake were being destroyed rapidly.

This particular species of the weed, called Phragmites
karka, had no documented use. Thus, removing the weed
meant pumping scarce funds into something that had no
tangible returns. Once removed, the weeds could only be left
to decay along the banks, producing an offensive odor.

Thus, the CDA wanted to investigate if some practical
use could be found for the weed, so that the local fishermen
could be incentivized to remove them regularly.

Dr Raina asked us to visit the lake, collect samples and
investigate various biological and physical properties of the
weed.

After investigating the properties and going through a
lot of research papers on the subject, we decided that the
best use for the weed was probably as biomass for a biogas
plant. So, we set up a pilot biogas plant in the lab and started
conducting experiments to ascertain the economical viability
of using Phragmites karka for the production of biogas."

The results were less than satisfactory.

"The weed was largely made up of hard cellulose. So, it
took much longer than agricultural or civic waste to putrefy
and the gas yield was low. Therefore, the cost per unit of the
gas would have been much higher than the alternatives. It

worked out to be ₹ 70 per unit of gas with Phragmites karka, as against the average figure of ₹ 45 per unit with most other organic waste."

However, the team did not give up. "We really expected the biogas solution to work and continued with the project even after the end of the summer break and into the next semester. We tried tinkering with a lot of variables to optimize the yield, but all our efforts met with disappointment. After sulking for some time, we started to explore other alternatives.

Then, in one eureka moment, it struck us that since the weed's cellulose content is high, it could be a good candidate for making paper."

At that time, the team had no idea about the paper-making process or the challenges involved. So, they started researching the industrial paper-making process.

"The industrial paper-making process is quite sophisticated. Once a tree is cut down, it goes to a mill, where it is debarked and then chipped by a series of blades. These chips are then ground into finer powder. The powder is heated under high pressure for a long time in a vat with water and chemicals such as caustic soda and sodium sulfate to make it into slurry known as pulp. In the final stages, additives such as starch, china clay, talc and calcium carbonate are added to the pulp to improve the strength and brightness of the paper. The pulp slurry is sprayed onto a huge flat wire screen. The fibers bond as the water drains out. The paper is then pressed between rolls, which squeezes out more water and makes for a smooth surface. Heated rollers then dry the paper, which is cut and rolled into sheets.

We had to implement a scaled-down version for laboratory experimentation. Unfortunately, the kind of equipment required for the purpose was not available in our laboratory and we had little financial means to get it. So, we made the equipment ourselves."

They grind the weed into a fine paste and mix the paste with water. The slurry thus created is treated with a host of biological enzymes in a specially designed bioreactor for a specified number of hours. Even the bleaching is achieved via the use of appropriate enzymes.

"Not only does our technology convert ecologically disastrous weeds into paper, and thereby, save wood, it also saves the environment from hazardous chemicals, because it does not involve chemical processes. The biological enzymes are biodegradable and can be recycled.

Because the weed grows very fast (it reaches the same density within one-and-a-half months of being weeded) and has no alternative use, it is quite inexpensive. Thus, the cost of the paper produced is one-third of that made from wood pulp. The quality of paper, in terms of strength, finish, smoothness and brightness, is as good as the conventional paper. It can be used for both writing and printing."

This proprietary system has been perfected over several iterations and the team has applied for a process patent for it.

"We have also found that this weed has good phytore-mediation (removal of organic pollutants and toxic heavy metals from the soil by plants) potential. Thus, growing the weed in areas where industrial effluents have caused soil pollution would ensure regeneration of soil. The soil can then be reclaimed for safe commercial agriculture."

In 2012, they applied for the India Innovation Initiative (I3) organized by Confederation of Indian Industries (CII) in association with Agilent Technologies. They were chosen among a select few from across the country to present their technology at a conference at IIT Delhi and also pitch to prospective investors.

"We didn't have money to go to Delhi by air, so we booked train tickets from Bhubaneswar to Kolkata, and then from Kolkata to Delhi. It was a long journey and we were scheduled to reach New Delhi by 5 AM. That would leave us with just enough time to go to our hotel room, dress up and reach IIT Delhi by 10 AM."

However, an innovator's journey is never without hurdles. "The journey was smooth until Kanpur. Around 10 PM, as the train halted at Kanpur station, a technical problem caused it to get delayed. There was no clear estimate of when the train would resume its journey; so, we kept waiting nervously. But as the clock struck midnight, we started to panic. It seemed like fate was against us.

Finally, at 1 AM, we boarded another train bound for Delhi. We didn't have a ticket and convinced the TTE (traveling ticket examiner) to help us. But it was already too late. By the time we reached IIT Delhi, all the other participants had already put up their posters and were interacting with the judges and the investors. It was quite disappointing to have traveled so far and missed the opportunity to interact with some of the well-known faces of the country's technology industry.

As we proceeded to the presentation, we could see that we were much less experienced than most of our competitors, who were much better prepared.

During the presentation, we were quizzed on several aspects of our work. We had printed a few business cards on our paper to present to the judges. They could not believe that it was not normal paper. They tried writing on it, dipped it in water and even tore it to check the strength.

We could easily address the queries on the technical aspects, but had little idea about the business aspects. We had never made a formal business plan. Because the investors were primarily interested in the business strategy and market potential, we were pretty confident that this was the end for us.

When the results were announced, to our great surprise, we found ourselves placed second. We received ₹ 30,000 as cash prize, but more importantly, we gained a lot of confidence. It dawned on us that we were doing great work and it was worth pursuing with even more vigor."

The team then applied to the DST–Lockheed Martin India Innovation Growth Program 2013 and was selected among the top 50 from across the country. "We were offered a week-long grooming workshop on technology commercialization and entrepreneurship before the final presentation. The workshop was held in Goa in April 2013, under the tutelage of faculty from Stanford Business School. It was extremely useful while facing the international panel of judges at the competition. We perfected our pitch for investors and got to interact with and learn from fellow participants.

We performed better than our expectations at the competition and were awarded a gold medal and a cash prize of ₹ 1 lakh. We were also offered an opportunity to go to Silicon Valley, along with nine other teams, to interact with investors and technologists there.

The catch was that only one of us could go to Silicon Valley. We were a bit dejected, because it would be unfair for only one of us to go when all of us had worked on the technology."

However, the teammates nominated Anurag to go on their behalf.

"The team members said that any one of them being there was as good as every one of them being there, because the learning would eventually be passed onto others as well.

Their selflessness was inspiring and made us stronger as a team," Anurag says.

However, the journey to the US was not as smooth as expected, he recalls. "I was to fly from Bhubaneswar to Delhi at 2 PM on August 24, 2013, to catch a flight to San Francisco on the night of the 24th. There was no news of the visa until the day before. I was very worried, but was in constant touch with the concerned people at FICCI, who were trying to do everything possible at their end. I received a call from the US consulate at 12:30 PM on the 24th; my passport was ready to be collected with the visa stamped, with just one-and-a-half hours remaining for my flight to Delhi. I immediately cancelled the ticket and FICCI booked another flight for me, scheduled to leave Bhubaneswar at 7 PM.

Because I had not been sure of getting the visa on time, I was yet to pack my bags. I rushed to my hostel and packed whatever clothes I had into a bag. I did not have many warm clothes, because Bhubaneswar is not as cold as San Francisco, but that was the last thing on my mind. I rushed directly to the airport after collecting the passport and was just in time for my flight to Delhi. It was my first flight ever and I was to fly almost continuously for the next 24 hours."

The journey was completely worth the anxiety, Anurag discovered. "The reception in Silicon Valley was amazing. We were being hosted by Stanford as a part of the Stanford Global Innovation Program and there were young innovators from around the globe. The program had been running for the last few years and we were the first batch of participants from India.

There were so many events planned for us and the treatment was simply outstanding. For the first time,

I realized that innovators could earn so much respect and recognition.

We were also taken to the campuses of Google, NASA and several technology start-ups and incubators, so that we could learn from the start-up culture in Silicon Valley. We got to interact with a lot of Indian technopreneurs via the Silicon Valley chapter of TiE. It was a truly amazing experience.

After returning, our team got felicitated by our university. We were offered incubation at the technology incubator within the university. The local media also praised us.

There is now a big shift in the attitude of students at our university toward research. Earlier, nobody did any projects or internships. Now, they are so inspired that almost everyone seems to be seeking to do a research project."

Anurag shares the team's future plans. "Currently, we are trying to scale up paper production from the laboratory to industrial scale. There are challenges involved in scaling up, such as loss of efficiency, that is, lower yield and increased duration of the process. We are trying to fix those issues now.

We are also working toward modeling the business as B2B rather than B2C, that is, supplying pulp to paper-making companies, rather than making paper and paper products and selling those to the end user.

We hope our efforts bear fruit and we are able to hit the market as soon as we complete our engineering degree."

For the Innovator in You

"All you can do is try your level best and leave everything else to God. Sometimes things work out, sometimes they do not, but you should learn from both success and failure. Do not be disappointed by failures. Remember what Thomas Edison said in response to the question on how he felt after failing 100 times before inventing the light bulb – 'It was not 100 failures; it was a 100-step process'."

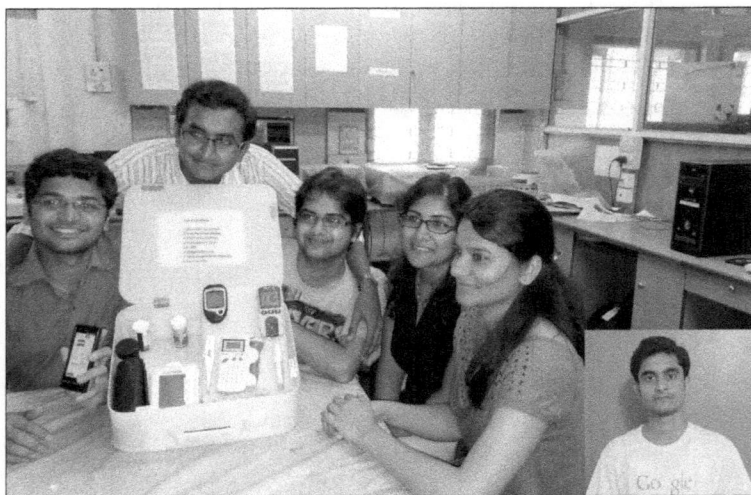

CareMother Team with the kit – (L to R) Shantanu Pathak, Swapnil Kokade, Vaibhav Tidke, Dr Shital Somani, Dr Shital Munde and Aditya Kulkarni (inset)

CareMother Testing Kit and Digital Platform for Providing Pregnancy Care

India holds the dubious distinction of having the highest number of pregnancy-related deaths in the world each year. According to a 2010 UN report, 19% (that is, almost 1 in 5) of global pregnancy-related deaths happened in India. This means that 56,000 mothers die in India every year, that is, 150 every day.

The gravity of the situation can be understood by looking at the next four countries on the list of pregnancy-related deaths by country: Nigeria – 14%, Democratic Republic of Congo – 5%, Pakistan – 4% and Sudan – 3.5%.

The maternal mortality rate, that is, the number of maternal deaths per 100,000 live births, stands at 200 for India. The same number is 50 times lower for Italy at just 4. Even China, with comparable demographic and economic status, has a much lower rate – 45 deaths per 100,000 live births.

The leading causes of maternal mortality include high blood pressure during pregnancy, severe bleeding and infections. Most of these complications can be avoided or handled without loss of life, if there is regular monitoring of high-risk pregnancies and timely medical aid is made available in emergency situations.

Unfortunately, despite several rural health schemes, access to good medical infrastructure and trained medical practitioners is limited to the cities. Mothers in rural parts of the country still have poor access to healthcare.

However, where the government has failed, a few young technologists are determined to make a difference.

Shantanu Pathak, an electronics engineer, started an informal group in 2008 called Science for Society; the aim was to bring together like-minded people to develop technologies for solving basic social problems. At that time, he was a second-year student at Lokmanya Tilak College of Engineering, Navi Mumbai.

From the beginning, the group's focus was to bring in people from different backgrounds to conduct interdisciplinary product-related research. As a result, a most unusual mix of people came together to create the most unusual results.

While his teammates were away, presenting their invention at a conference in Pune, Shantanu took me through the inspirational journey of Science for Society.

"Initially, Science for Society began as an NGO. Anybody who had a passion for technology and wanted to use his knowledge for the greater good was welcome. Some people contributed ideas and others helped with the execution. There were those who worked for a short time and those who stayed forever.

Among those who swore their permanent allegiance to Science for Society were Swapnil Kokade, Vaibhav Tidke, Aditya Kulkarni, Dr Shital Somani and Dr Shital Munde.

In the beginning, the focus was more on renewable energy. We designed some manually powered LED lighting devices and a manually driven UV disinfection system for water purification. Water purification kits were even installed in a few rural schools. We also made a solar-powered conduction dryer to dehydrate fruits and vegetables and increase their shelf life, thereby saving at least 33% of seasonal agro-products in areas that do not have access to reliable electricity. We were awarded the Mondialgo Engineering Award in 2009 for the dryer by Daimler AG (the manufacturers of Mercedes cars) in association with UNESCO. We were invited to Stuttgart, Germany to receive the award worth 20,000 euros.

Another solar-energy-based device we made during this period was an egg incubator, which not only saved the cost of electricity, but was also eight times cheaper as compared to the conventional electric egg incubator."

The team obtained patents for each of those devices.

The team's focus soon shifted to healthcare.

Shantanu describes the team's motivations. "I always wanted to do something in healthcare. I come from a very small town called Risod, located in the Washim district of Maharashtra. I lost my father when I was just 12 years old. It happened suddenly and the doctors could never ascertain the reasons. Despite the era of economic hardships that followed, my elder brother and mother ensured that I got the best education possible. I always felt that if my father could have had regular health checkups, he would probably be alive today. Thus, I wanted to do something to improve healthcare access for the masses. My other teammates were also from small towns and they, too, felt strongly about rural healthcare access.

Dr Shital Somani is a dentist; she suggested we work on an automated dental X-ray machine. Because the oral cavity is comprised of bony and soft tissues, dental treatment needs an X-ray for diagnosis at all stages of the treatment process. All dentists have their own dental X-ray setup, and roughly 200,000 dental X-rays are taken in India every day. In order to develop the X-ray films, a series of dark-room chemical reactions need to be performed manually. The process is time-consuming and requires frequently changing chemicals; still, the quality of films is inconsistent. The aim was to automate the dental X-ray processor, so that it reduces time taken and chemical usage and results in better quality of films.

A few imported X-ray processors are available in the market, but they cost between ₹ 50,000–300,000 and every Indian dentist cannot afford them. These machines also have maintenance problems and are bulky, making them unsuitable for rural mobile clinics.

Thus, the challenge was to make a portable, almost zero-maintenance, low-cost device.

X-ray processing is a solid–liquid multiphase reaction process. Keeping this in mind, we designed a novel solid fluid reactor that uses only the optimum amount of chemicals. The reactor was also provided with a vibrator to carry out uniform mixing and accelerate the rate of reaction. A series of chemical reactions and drying are carried out in a sequential manner and the entire process is controlled by a microcontroller. We also used an air exclusion chamber to prevent oxidation and contamination."

Shantanu states that these innovations helped them achieve a reduction of 75% in the consumption of environmentally hazardous chemicals. Moreover, it was possible to use the machine in a non-air conditioned or dusty environment. The machine did not use any moving parts and required so little energy that it could be operated on a battery of modest capabilities. Thus, it was easy to maintain and did not need electricity to work.

"Its cost worked out to be just ₹ 5,000 and it did not require any trained labor to operate," Shantanu adds.

"The project received a lot of attention and appreciation. We were featured in the Dell Social Innovation Challenge in 2010 and applied for a patent soon thereafter."

By this time, Shantanu had completed his graduation. "I was sure I wanted to keep inventing something to make lives better for the underprivileged. At the same time, it was a reality that I needed a job to save enough to put into my experiments and also to support my family.

I really liked telecommunications; so, I took up a job with a Chinese telecom equipment manufacturer, ZTE Telecom. The job required me to relocate to Shenzen, China. Shital joined a management program in Mumbai and got married. Aditya moved to the Indian Space Research Organization (ISRO) for a job and eventually to National University of Singapore to pursue a PhD program in Computer Science. Vaibhav and Swapnil were still pursuing their respective programs at the Institute of Chemical Technology (ICT), Mumbai."

The future of Science for Society was uncertain at this point. "We had some really good technologies, but some of the people who had worked on the projects had left and we were not sure if we should commercialize the technologies without them. Moreover, we were not really business-oriented.

Despite being in different parts of the world, we kept in touch via the internet. Around the same time, Dr Shital Munde's elder sister got pregnant. Her last two pregnancies had ended in miscarriages, first due to high blood pressure (gestational hypertensive disorder or pregnancy induced hypertension) and the second due to excessive bleeding. This time too, it was a high-risk pregnancy.

Shital, being a doctor herself, started recording the blood pressure and urinary protein levels every six hours, which is the standard practice in such cases. The process was uncomfortable, because the samples needed to be taken to a pathology laboratory every few hours.

In one of our brainstorming sessions, we realized that Shital's sister was lucky that she had a doctor in the family and could be monitored 24x7. Many others were not as fortunate, for they either did not have access to a doctor or could not afford frequent testing and medical consultations.

When we came across the statistics on maternal mortality, we were absolutely determined to do something about it.

We figured out that there were two parts to the problem. First, to make a portable non-invasive testing kit which could save the patient the trouble of going to a lab for testing and allow any untrained person to record the readings; and second, to make the patient's test results accessible to a doctor, who could then advise the patient accordingly."

The team began on the hardware first. "We divided the responsibilities and started working from wherever we were, conducting meetings and discussions online. We focused on our respective jobs or academics in the day and worked late into the night on the project. The experience with telecom equipment came handy during this time.

We wanted to make sure the kit could test all the key pregnancy-related parameters, and yet, be light and inexpensive. Some of the instruments available were already quite portable, but others were not. Also, some were too expensive. We had to redesign some of the testing equipment to make it lighter or cost-effective. For instance, the weighing scale itself weighs about half a kilogram and is difficult to carry around. We had to redesign it to fit into the box of the kit; we also ensured that the whole kit, weighing scale included, did not weigh more than a couple of kilograms. Usually, the fetal heart rate (FHR) meter takes up to 10 minutes to give a reading, which consumes a lot of battery. We designed the FHR meter in our kit to give a reading in just a couple of minutes, so the battery lasts longer.

As the work on this project increased, we realized its potential in ushering a healthcare revolution in many developing countries. We started considering pursuing this project full-time and devoting ourselves to taking it to the market."

After a year with ZTE in China, Shantanu resigned from the job. He decided to come back to India and pursue activities at Science for Technology full-time.

"In 2011, we incorporated Science for Society as a company by the name of Science for Technology Techno-Services Pvt Ltd and took up a small office in Dadar. The project got a name – CareMother, and we started developing an app to link the patient with the doctor. At the same time, we started work on a business model in order to make it commercially viable.

During that time, in order to support ourselves, some of us did tuitions and other part-time jobs, but we did not let the work suffer.

We did an extensive ground survey to identify the pain points, ascertain the features that would be useful for end users and price points the users were comfortable with. It took us about ten months to get the app and business plan ready."

This is how CareMother works. The community health worker can take the portable CareMother kit to the patient's home and conduct vital pregnancy-related tests, such as weight, height, temperature, blood pressure, blood hemoglobin, FHR and fundal height (the size of the uterus, which is used to assess fetal growth and development during pregnancy; it is measured in centimeters, from the top of the mother's uterus to the top of her pubic bone). The health worker then enters the data into the CareMother app and saves it. The data is uploaded automatically to the CareMother server as soon as an internet connection is available.

"So, even if there is no mobile internet, the health worker can save several patients' data, which will be uploaded when she reaches a location where wireless or other internet connectivity is available. Once the data is uploaded, the app has built-in analytics to ascertain if any of the tested parameters are out of the safety range. The data is also immediately available to the doctor who is monitoring that patient. Thus, the system provides patients with remote access to the doctor.

The community health workers can charge a small fee, around ₹ 100, for testing services. This would earn them a good livelihood. Also, the doctors can monitor patients remotely for a very small lump sum fee, say a couple of thousands, for the entire pregnancy. By paying ₹ 10,000 to access the CareMother platform, doctors can increase their reach, that too with little additional burden on their clinic/ hospital infrastructure or their time. Moreover, because patients usually go to the same doctor for delivery who has been advising them during pregnancy, there is an added incentive for doctors.

Owing to a stressful life that requires balancing the home and workplace, more and more urban women are falling prey to pregnancy-related complications. The system comes to the rescue of urban mothers as well. Educated women can use the kit to perform the tests on their own and upload the data using their smartphones. Thus, they need not make frequent trips to the lab and the doctor; this saves time and helps them avoid the discomfort of urban travel during pregnancy.

The patient's history is recorded in the app and can easily be accessed by the physician whenever required.

The app also provides important information to mothers on nutrition, exercise and family planning; informs the mother when she should visit her doctor; and lets patients use a scale to quantify the intensity of symptoms such as morning sickness or pain for the doctor to assess. Moreover, for other relevant information, the patient can even choose to leave voice messages for the doctor. Currently, the app can be accessed in three languages – Hindi, English and Marathi. We are in the process of adding more Indian languages to it.

We have put a lot of things together in a way that allows us to address the needs of pregnancy care very effectively."

In early 2013, the CareMother team started a pilot program in association with Doctors For You (DFY), a pan-India humanitarian organization which focuses on providing medical care to vulnerable communities during crisis and non-crisis situations. CareMother had 100 patients within four months, 10 of which belonged to the high-risk category. This helped them get user feedback.

The response was amazing. DFY found the system so easy and useful that the pilot program that started at one of their centers was extended to others. Soon, several organizations from across the country started approaching us."

NGOs such as Pragya from Jammu and Kashmir and Sri Sathya Sai Central Trust, Andhra Pradesh, as well as private hospitals such as Kamineni Hospitals, Hyderabad, have expressed the desire to use CareMother to reach out to rural patients in their respective areas.

Government departments are not far behind. Sector Wide Approach to Strengthen Health (SWASTH), a healthcare initiative by the Bihar Government, has approached the CareMother team for help. Non-profit healthcare research organizations such as Health Management and Research Institute (HMRI) have also sought a partnership.

The project has received international acclaim as well. The UK government awarded a grant to the CareMother team under the UK–India Education and Research Initiative. The grant enabled the team to travel to the UK and network with leading experts on m-health (heath care delivery via mobile technologies).

"In the UK, the government-funded National Health System (NHS) is under severe pressure due to demand–supply gap. Therefore, even advanced countries such as the UK are looking to m-health for better healthcare delivery."

CareMother was also awarded a gold medal under the DST–Lockheed Martin India Innovation Growth Program. The team received mentorship from Stanford Business School and a chance to meet investors in Silicon Valley. They were also chosen to be part of a USAID–FICCI innovation support program called Millennium Alliance.

In September 2013, they were adjudged the winners under the Public Service category at the 2013 Yahoo! Innovation Jockey. The Yahoo! homepage saluted their efforts to make life better for mothers around the world.

About 30 million pregnancies occur in India annually, of which almost 75% are in rural areas. Therefore, the CareMother team plans to reach out to the 150,000 rural health care centers spread over 5,000 *talukas* in India over the next four years.

They also plan to add other m-health offerings such as CareChild, a similar product aimed at preventing early childhood diseases and deaths. (India also leads the world in the number of deaths of children below 5 years of age, accounting for a quarter of the worldwide figure.)

The team also plans to revive past projects for commercialization. Dr Shital Somani and Vaibhav now handle technology commercialization and business development for the company. They are also considering using their expertise in solar energy to implement a charging system for the CareMother kit.

With young and determined social technopreneurs at the helm, the future of rural India is bound to change for the better.

For the Innovator in You

"Innovation and the entrepreneurship environment in the country are growing. Venture capital funding and grants are more easily available than in the past; so, it is the best time to put your ideas into action. Figure out the problems that people face and try to ascertain how they can be solved in the easiest possible manner.

Convincing yourself to chuck a job and pursue your idea full-time will be the most difficult challenge. Believe that in case things do not work out, you will still find a job, probably better than your last job. It is a good idea to get some part-time work in the initial phases, so that you do not face financial pressure.

Last but not the least, know your weaknesses, and do not be stubborn. Be open-minded and adaptive enough to change your problem statement and the strategy, based on the feedback."

Chinmay Deodhar

Dual-Purpose Laparoscopic Surgery Instrument

It is foolhardy to expect an automotive engineer to create a high-precision surgical instrument. But not if that automotive engineer happens to be Chinmay Deodhar!

Despite having no formal background in medical sciences, Chinmay developed an instrument that eases a surgeon's work during the skill-intensive laparoscopic surgery.

Laparoscopic surgery, also called minimally invasive or keyhole surgery, is a modern technique in which abdominal surgeries are performed through small incisions, 5-10 mm in diameter.

Trocar, a three-edged triangular medical device with a hollow tube and a seal, is placed through the incisions. The trocar then functions as a portal for subsequent insertion of other specially designed (with diameters of less than 5 mm) instruments into the body cavity for specific purposes, such as viewing, cutting, grasping and cauterizing (sealing a blood vessel via the application of heat).

Doctors use a sophisticated camera with an inbuilt light source, called the laparoscope, to access a magnified view of the body cavity while performing the surgery. Thus, laparoscopy requires very good hand-eye coordination and great surgical precision.

Usually, only one instrument can be inserted at a time through a trocar. Thus, the doctor may make multiple incisions if various tools are to be used together, or may need to pull one tool out to insert another.

This process can be time-consuming, tedious and exhausting. It also endangers the patient, because the doctor's focus is more on removing and reinserting different tools than on the procedure.

Surgeons across the world face this challenge daily while performing laparoscopic surgical procedures. However, 25-year-old Chinmay Deodhar's efforts may soon provide a much-needed solution.

Chinmay was born and brought up in Pune. His father, a software professional, instilled a passion for technology in him. While Chinmay was always a bright student, he excelled at chess too and played the game at the state level, before the IIT bug bit him.

Chinmay was keenly interested in designing mechanical objects. He excelled at wood crafting in school, and even made a wooden Ackermann Steering Mechanism (a very famous steering system) at that time.

Thus, after acing the IIT-JEE in 2005, and despite having a plethora of options, he chose a new course being offered at IIT Madras that year – a dual-degree program comprising a Bachelor of Technology degree in Engineering Design and Masters of Technology in Automotive Engineering.

"The course was multidisciplinary and offered a chance to learn a lot about electronics, mechanical engineering, material science and industrial design. The moment I read about the course description in the counseling brochure, I knew that this was the course for me. The design part entailed a lot of clay modeling and sketching, and was thus a good cross between science and arts. Thus, the course fostered a lot of creativity.

In the first couple of years at IIT, we were exposed to the world of programming and software development. In those days, most phones ran Java-based applications and games. I had a Nokia 6233 and used to play Macromedia Flash-based animated games on it.

During the summer break of the second year, I came back to Pune. A lot of my friends who were nearing their graduation were eagerly preparing for the GRE to go to the US for higher studies. Some of them had even enrolled at Dilip Oak's Academy, which is a leading institute in Pune for GRE/GMAT preparation."

Preparing for the GRE requires memorizing a lot of words for vocabulary-based questions. Flash cards are often used for this, each of which contains the word, its pronunciation, meaning, usage and a methodology to remember it.

"I thought that if the vocabulary flash cards could be made available through a mobile phone application, people would be able to carry the cards with them easily and go through them anywhere, at any time.

Over the next few days, I developed a crude version of the game, which had information on just a few words." Chinmay named the application *Quickword*.

"Once the first version was ready, I decided to pitch the idea to Dilip Oak and see if he would be interested in buying it for his students."

Even though it was a demo version, Dilip Oak was more than impressed and offered to buy the fully developed version for ₹ 1.5 lakh.

"I was thrilled. ₹ 1.5 lakh is a huge amount of money when you are in college. I realized that if you applied your knowledge to develop solutions that help make people's life easier, you can earn a lot of money. So, the entrepreneur in me started taking root.

A few months later, around mid-2007, many mobile companies announced internet data plans as cheap as 10 kb for 10 paise. Along with a friend, I started developing a J2ME application, named Lypas, which would let a user send an SMS to any other Lypas user, much like what Whatsapp and other such applications do today. 10 kb would permit sending as many as 100 short messages, making the communication almost free.

While we were still working on Lypas, we learned about IIM Ahmedabad's iAccelerator program and applied for it." iAccelerator is a technology business incubation program offered by IIM Ahmedabad's Centre for Innovation, Incubation and Entrepreneurship (CIIE).

A few weeks later, to our surprise, we were selected for iAccelerator. It was almost like a dream come true. Under the program, we were taught the basics of accounting and start-up financing at IIM Ahmedabad and had interactive sessions with several successful technology entrepreneurs."

However, that venture did not take off, because distributing the app was difficult. "Unlike today, there was no app store back then and the penetration of internet-enabled phones was low. Thus, despite the availability of cheap, low-speed internet data plans, internet consumption on phones was hardly taking off. Downloading the app on the PC and then transferring the file to the phone via Bluetooth or data cable for installation was a painful task that only a few users were ready to undertake."

Chinmay moved on to other interests. "In the fourth year of my engineering degree, I began a six-month industrial training at Precision Automation & Robotics India Limited (PARI) in Pune, a company that specializes in manufacturing industrial automation systems for the automotive industry."

At that time, the company was entering the medical devices arena and Chinmay was assigned to visit hospitals and observe laparoscopic procedures. He was to study the instruments used, in order to gather technical know-how on their design and fabrication.

"On the very first hospital visit, I watched a laparoscopic abdominal cancer operation. I was surprised that there were four types of graspers alone. It was easy to realize that the surgeons had difficulties replacing one instrument with the other.

As I delved deeper, I got hooked to the subject. I spent the rest of the internship trying to understand different aspects of the instruments' design and usage. One of my uncles, a laparoscopic surgeon in Pune, guided me on the finer aspects of instrument design and the problems faced by surgeons.

All this while, I wondered if two or more instruments could be combined into one. Initially, I wanted to combine the cauterizer, scissors and grasper. However, with further research, I realized that it would be difficult to do that, because other tissues that are not to be cauterized need to be shielded from the heat via insulation."

It was decided that the most feasible solution would be to combine a grasper and scissors.

"The design was ready by the end of April 2010 and I got it prototyped via 3D printing. Over the next few months, I received feedback on the instrument from several surgeons and refined it further. In June 2010, just after graduating from IIT Madras, I filed for a provisional patent through a Pune-based lawyer."

Chinmay now wanted to license the intellectual property (IP) of the device to a big medical devices company. "However, I had no idea how I could go about selling my IP and who the likely buyers would be.

Through extensive Google searches and a few industry insiders, I came to know about a small town in south Germany, Tuttlingen. It is a town of just 33,000 people, but 50% of the world's surgical instruments are made here. About 600 companies in Tuttlingen, ranging from one-man operations to multinationals, specialize in surgical instruments."

Chinmay did not know anybody who could connect him to the senior managers of these companies, but he did not want to give up. Therefore, he decided to go to Germany and contact them on his own.

"I had secured a job at the automotive division of Eaton, a Pune-based conglomerate, via campus placements. The job was to start in August. Meanwhile, I had some time and decided to go to Germany. Luckily, my parents supported me and helped with the finances.

One of my cousins lived in Basel, Switzerland, which is just a two-hour train ride from Tuttlingen. I stayed with him and bought a bicycle. Every day, I would cycle to the Basel train station and take the train to Tuttlingen. At Tuttlingen, I would mount the bicycle once again. I would then go looking for the offices of the companies whose locations I had marked on a Google map printout that I carried with me.

I would knock at the door of the so-called *Medizin Techniks* and introduce myself to whoever answered. People in Germany are accustomed to receiving people with a proper appointment, so most of the time, I was turned down immediately. However, some people would take me in out of curiosity that some "young lad" had traveled all the way from India to try and sell a patent.

A few of them gave me a chance to explain the novelty of the product, how it works, how it would benefit the surgeons and the financials involved. Though they would give me just five minutes, once I began, they would be so engrossed that the meeting would easily stretch to half an hour or so.

In a few weeks, I managed to reach out to about 40 companies, but only four or five of them showed any interest.

One of them, instead of purchasing the patent, offered me a job. However, I had to decline the offer because that was not my aim. Another company wanted to apply for the German government's Fraunhofer Grant to help with the commercialization of the product, which was a long-drawn and uncertain process.

At one of the companies, where I was not allowed to meet anyone from the management, I had just left my card and other details at the reception. I never expected the card or the details to reach the concerned person, and thus, almost forgot about it. However, as luck would have it, I received a mail from them the same week, expressing profound interest. It was a mark of recognition and gave me a lot of confidence that my product was worth the effort that I spent on it.

They called me for a meeting and were visibly impressed. However, they wanted me to prepare a to-scale model of the device in surgical stainless steel before they could make a further decision.

So, I came back to Pune and started to work on the to-scale model. I also joined my job at Eaton. With the job, I could work on the model only on the weekends, which slowed the progress considerably. Meanwhile, I received news that I had been chosen for the Stanford India Biodesign Fellowship."

Funded by the DBT at the Ministry of Science and Technology, Government of India, the Stanford India Biodesign (SIB) Fellowship Program is a one-year research program administered in collaboration with IIT Delhi, All India Institute of Medical Sciences (AIIMS) and Stanford University, USA. The program is run in partnership with the Indo-US Science and Technology Forum (IUSSTF) and aims to develop the next generation of medical technology innovators in India. Fellows work in a multidisciplinary team, joining other innovators from engineering, medical and business backgrounds to help solve healthcare-related problems. They spend the first six months at Stanford University and the next six months in India.

"I had decided to go for the program; so, I left the job one-and-a-half months after joining. The program was to begin in January 2011, and there were still a couple of months to go, just sufficient time for me to complete work on the final to-scale model.

I kept in touch with the German company throughout this period and even after landing in the US. I also hired an agent to represent me in Germany and work out the modalities.

Once in the US, I started approaching the US companies as well and attended various industrial expositions related to surgical devices.

By May 2011, a couple of American companies were also interested. Negotiations then began with all the interested parties and continued even after I came back to India.

The professors at Stanford helped a lot with drafting the agreement. Participants in the program who had prior experience in selling patents dispensed very useful advice on how much to disclose, when and to whom. Thus, the Stanford connection came in handy.

Finally, a deal was sealed in November 2011 with Intuitive Surgical Inc., a California-based, NASDAQ-listed MNC known for its robotic surgical systems.

It will take some time for the product to come into the market, as necessary clinical trials and FDA approvals are required for that."

At Stanford, Chinmay worked on a device to prevent birth asphyxia, a medical condition in which a newborn does not receive enough oxygen before, during or just after birth. Birth asphyxia affects five out of 100 babies and can lead to disabilities or death, because the brain and other organs fail to receive enough oxygen. Each year, one million newborns die because of this condition. Timely medical intervention via a procedure called basic neo-natal resuscitation can save infants with birth asphyxia. The procedure involves pushing air into the newborn's lungs through a tightly closed mouth by using special pumps. The process requires skill and expertise, because the air pressure should neither be too high nor too low. Such expertise is often not available in most Indian rural hospitals.

Chinmay was named among the top 35 Indian innovators by MIT Technology Review in 2013. He now works as a design consultant for some of the leading German and American medical devices companies. He has also incorporated a company in Pune by the name of Croleon Innovation Labs and is working on devices to help with robot-assisted and spinal surgeries. While he continues to carve out his niche in the high-precision medical devices industry, which is largely dominated by Western companies, he has not forgotten his social dues. As a gesture of giving back to his alma mater, Chinmay has sponsored an endowment fund at IIT Madras to support innovation. The endowment provides scholarships to students involved in innovation at the institute and enables them carry their work forward, thus ensuring that the country gets many more Chinmays.

For the Innovator in You

"Be very careful in protecting your IPR. You should file an Indian patent as soon as the product is ready and then apply for a PCT, which can then be followed by country-wise patents, as required.

If you are looking to sell your patent, it is important to select a reliable and reputed agent. Genuine agents never ask for upfront payment to represent you; they take a percentage of the deal they get you. You should be wary of any agent who asks you to pay upfront. The percentage-based commission also keeps the agent motivated to work in your best interests.

It is important to experience rejection, because without it, success would never seem as sweet. Reaching out to those German companies and getting rejected repeatedly taught me much more than what 100 MBA degrees could have. So, do not be risk-averse and do not shy away from rejection. The difference between a stumbling block and a stepping stone is how high you raise your foot."

Arunachalam Muruganantham

Low-Cost Sanitary Pad Making Machine

A study by AC Nielsen in 2010 revealed that of the 355 million menstruating women in India, only 12% used sanitary napkins. Moreover, in rural India, just 2% of menstruating women used sanitary napkins.

Unable to afford a napkin, women in poor households turn to cloth rags. Cotton rags used for the purpose are usually washed and reused, sometimes while they are yet to dry completely, which increases the likelihood of the rag being infested with bacteria. Some even poorer women, who may not have enough sarees to tear a few of them for rags, even use ash, husk, sand or a combination of these. This increases their risk of contracting bacterial, viral, worm and fungal infections in the reproductive tract, pelvic inflammation and even cervical cancer.

Menstruation in India has traditionally been associated with myths and taboos. It is never discussed openly and menstruating women are often barred from religious rituals. In fact, the subject is so hushed up that women find it difficult to talk about their menstrual problems to their husbands and even their mothers-in-law, forcing them to face these problems alone.

This is exactly what Arunachalam Muruganantham encountered when he got married. But unlike others, he resolved to find a solution.

Muruganantham was born in a village near Coimbatore, Tamil Nadu. His father was a poor handloom weaver on the outskirts of the city that is known as the Manchester of South India for its cotton textile industry.

Muruganantham studied at a government school till Class X, after which he was forced to quit his education, because of his father's untimely death in a road accident.

Initially, his mother made ends meet by selling her jewelry, household furniture and other valuables, but at last, Muruganantham was forced to leave school and find a job with a local welder. He did not know welding at that time; so, he was hired as an assistant for just ₹ 2 per day. Meanwhile, his mother also found work as farm labor for a measly ₹ 3 per day, and together, they somehow carved out an existence.

By his late teens, Muruganantham became adept at welding and even started copying his sister's intricate *rangoli* designs for gates and window grills. At that time, most other welders would do only simple circular and rectangular patterns. Therefore, Muruganantham's designs became an instant hit and people came from far-flung areas to buy his gates and window grills.

"One fine day, the shop-owner, who was a drunkard and pretty old by now, offered me a deal. I was among the finest workers around, worked hard and was now old enough to handle things on my own; so, he believed I could run the workshop. He asked me to buy the workshop from him and run it on my own, while he could retire and drink his last few days away.

He asked for ₹ 60,000 which I did not have. So, he arranged for a moneylender to lend me the money. From a shop-floor worker, I directly went on to become the owner.

Over the next several years, I worked extremely hard to be able to pay back the principal and the interest.

Finally, when the workshop was earning decent returns, marriage proposals started pouring in. In 1998, I tied the knot.

One day, I saw my wife carrying something behind her back. When I asked her what she was hiding from me, she said it was a trivial matter that did not concern me.

When I insisted, she revealed what she was carrying – a blood-smeared rag. I understood what it was and suggested that she use a sanitary napkin instead. She retorted that though she knew about sanitary pads, using them would mean the family forgoing some other more important commodity such as milk, because our budget would not allow for both.

I doubted that something as simple as a sanitary napkin could stretch our budget so much. So, I went to a provision store nearby and asked for a packet of sanitary napkins. The shopkeeper was surprised to see a male asking for sanitary napkins. When he found out that I was newly married, he was very amused that I would help my wife with 'such issues'.

He wrapped the packet in a newspaper and handed it to me surreptitiously, as if it was contraband!

It was the first time I had held a sanitary napkin in my hand. It would have weighed less than 10 grams. The cost of 10 grams cotton was just 10 paise in those days; yet, the sanitary pad was about ₹ 3 per piece. I realized that lack of awareness was not the only reason for so many women in the village using husk, leaves or newspapers for the purpose. The cost was prohibitive for most daily-wage laborers."

Muruganantham thought of making a sanitary napkin for his wife.

"I got the finest cotton from a local shopkeeper, cut it to size, flattened it, wrapped it into a rayon cloth and gave it to my wife.

The next day, I asked for her feedback, but she was visibly irritated by my insistence on the subject. She said I would have to wait until next month, that is, the next menstrual cycle.

When she used it, she was extremely unhappy with it. She felt that she was much better-off with the rag. Yet, she would not say what was so unsatisfactory about the sanitary pad."

Every time he modified the napkin, he would have to wait for a month to get his wife's feedback. When she did give feedback, it was only to say that she was not satisfied, without giving any reasons. Thus, he had no idea where he was going wrong. His inquisitiveness and impatience were growing, as was his wife's anger at his 'stupid and perverted attempt to enter a woman's secret world.'

"I thought my sister would be more cooperative and open in sharing her opinion. So, I started pushing her to use my napkin as well. Unfortunately, she was even less forthcoming and barred me from entering her house, once she understood what I was up to.

After having failed with my family members, I turned to girls studying in a medical college. I thought they would be more open about the subject, as they were future doctors.

I contacted a few girls at the nearest medical college, which was 28 km away, and explained the situation. I would go to the medical college every month and give them the pads and ask for their opinion. To my surprise, even they were shy to talk about it.

In order to prevent embarrassing them, I started handing them a feedback sheet along with the pad. They had to answer the questions on the sheet with Yes/No responses and return the sheet to me.

One day, I saw a few of them filling out the responses on behalf of everyone. I knew this approach had also failed.

Something else was failing too – my marriage.

Small towns and villages are hotbeds of rumors. Everybody knows everybody else and people have little work except meddling in other's lives.

The village was abuzz with the news that I was hanging around the medical college gates. My wife, baffled by my frequent trips to the medical college, started suspecting that I was seeing some girl there. She confronted me one day, but because she was unhappy with my napkin project, I could not mention it. She was so furious that she left our house and went back to her parents. I tried to reason with her, but to no avail. After a few days, I got a divorce notice.

Despite everything, I continued to experiment. Now, I started to ask the girls at medical college to return the used napkins. I was not expecting them to cooperate and had even planned to bribe the garbage collector to get me the napkins from the garbage. However, my persuasion worked, and thankfully, I did not have to go that length.

I used to keep the collected napkins in a bin in a locked room and analyze them on Sundays, when my mother had gone to the fields.

One day, she returned early and saw me working with a few stained napkins on the table, while the room stank of rotting napkins.

She thought I had either gone mad or some spirit had possessed me. She packed her bags and left too. I had to now fend for myself. I needed a lot of emotional support at that time. I was completely broken."

Surprisingly, Muruganantham did not give up despite such strong opposition.

"It only strengthened my resolve further. I knew I had lost the trust of my wife and my mother; the only way to win it back was to complete the project successfully and prove that I was neither mad nor perverted. I knew that if I failed, I would not have failed just as an innovator, but also as a son and a husband. I had to win; there was no other way now.

I had lost so much, yet I had made little progress with the pads. In the absence of feedback from the girls, I decided to put on the sanitary napkin myself.

In order to replicate the uterus, I used a rubber bladder from a deflated soccer ball, filled it with goat's blood and added anti-coagulants to it. I connected a tube from the bladder to the sanitary pad which was tied to my hips between my legs. I squeezed the bladder every 20 minutes as I went about my daily activities.

I used to get goat's blood regularly from the butcher in the village, so rumors started that I was pursuing black magic. Some people even said that I was affected with sexually transmitted diseases.

Things came to such a pass that I decided to leave the village for good and move to Coimbatore."

After moving to Coimbatore, Muruganantham started approaching labs to identify, analyze and compare the components of his pads with those manufactured by MNCs.

The tests revealed that the crucial difference between his pads and those of the multinationals was the fiber used. While he used a single type of cotton, commercially manufactured napkins used a combination of several types of cotton that was blended with cellulose derived from the pulp of the bark of pine trees. This provided better retention than pure cotton.

"The tests were worth a few lakh rupees and ate into all my savings. The living expenses in Coimbatore were higher; so, I started working 10 hours each day at the workshop and even sold my blood at times to make ends meet. Even after working long hours in the workshop, I would devote at least two hours per day to my research.

I worked very hard to determine what made this cellulose so special, how it was manufactured and how it could be replicated using locally available material.

During the investigation, I found out that the cellulose extraction process required machines worth several crores. Thus, the technology created high barriers to entry for small players. It was obvious then that I had to create a sanitary napkin of the same quality without using cellulose.

Over the next two years, I perfected the blend of cotton and thickness of the pad by trial and error. I also developed all the machines required to process the cotton, and press and package it into usable pads.

Finally, in 2005, seven years after I had begun my quest for affordable sanitary napkins, I patented the product and the process with the help of National Innovation Foundation. I also sent my technology to IIT Madras for evaluation and their seal of approval, so that there is more credibility."

IIT Madras did not just approve it; they awarded it the Best Social Innovation of the Year. Soon, the local Tamil media was flush with news on how a school dropout was set to change the lives of millions of women across the country.

When the news of his success reached his wife and mother, both of them decided to come back. Many of the people, who had earlier ridiculed him, could not stop singing his praises now and would often tell him that they always knew that he would make it big one day.

"Everybody expected me to make a lot of money. I received offers from multinationals on several occasions to sell the technology to them for a hefty sum, but I declined each time.

I am the son of a poor handloom weaver and I have seen the worst of poverty. The struggle to create the sanitary pad took me through hell. If I could survive all that, I am sure I do not need so much money.

I lead a simple life and have learned to live with scarce resources. I am very happy with whatever I have, but I want to create opportunities to make life better for rural women."

For this purpose, he started Jayashree Industries, a company that manufactures the sanitary pad making machines. The machines are sold to women self-help groups in rural areas. The price of the machine depends on its manufacturing capacity, and varies from ₹ 75,000 for a machine that produces 500 pads per day to ₹ 200,000 for one that produces 3,000 per day. The women are trained to operate the machines, educate their prospective buyers about the benefits of the product and manage inventory and sales.

All raw materials are sourced locally. Each of the self-help groups sells the napkins under their own local brand name, which enhances their sense of identity, pride and independence. The napkins are sold door-to-door, which is convenient for users and saves them the embarrassment of asking for the product at a provision store. If a daily-wage earner would like to buy a single pad, the women sellers do not mind opening up the packet and selling a single piece. They even sell the pads in a barter exchange. Thus, while MNCs use a centralized and standardized marketing and distribution model for their branded sanitary napkins, these sanitary napkins are delivered through a multi-brand, decentralized, customizable model.

The raw material and processing costs ₹ 1 per pad and the labor and other overheads add another 50 paise. The pads are sold at ₹ 2 per piece, almost one-fifth of the price charged by most MNCs. The women in the self-help groups are able to earn ₹ 5,000-10,000 per month, depending on sales. This is much higher than the ₹ 2,000-3,000 they would make as agricultural laborers. Many of them can now afford to send their children to school.

The process involves grinding raw cotton bales into finer fibers in a grinding bucket. The ground cotton is then weighed and separated into 100 g piles, each of which is sufficient for 10 pads. The cotton is then put into rectangular molds. A pneumatic press is used to press three pads at a time. The pressed cotton pads are then attached to a plastic liner using super-bond glue. A very fine cloth is then wrapped around the pad and heat-sealed. The finished napkins are UV sterilized, put inside peel-off paper and packed. They are sold in packs of eight in a plastic bag that carries the local branding of the self-help group manufacturing them.

Today, the enterprise involves almost 10,000 rural women organized into 843 self-help groups, spread across 27 Indian states and some other developing countries such as Bhutan, Afghanistan, Bangladesh, Nigeria, Ethiopia, Uganda, Kenya, Zimbabwe and South Africa. So far, it is estimated that 3.5 million women have been converted to sanitary pad users by these self-help groups.

Muruganantham has also set up a sanitary pad making machine in an NGO-run girls' school in Anupshaher, Uttar Pradesh. Thus, girls enrolled in the school are educated about sexual hygiene and are also incentivized to not drop out of school, because they get to earn some money through making and selling sanitary napkins.

With help from the National Rural Health Mission, he has installed pad-vending machines in some areas, which dispense pads in exchange of a two-rupee coin.

In 2009, Muruganantham received a prize from President Pratibha Patil for his innovation. Since then, he has received scores of awards for inclusive innovation, social entrepreneurship, women empowerment and rural upliftment.

He is now a subject of case studies in management campuses across the world and often finds himself flying from one city to another, delivering talks at prestigious forums.

Until 2009, Muruganantham could not speak much English and relied on interpreters to deliver his talks around the world. However, because a lot is lost in translation, he decided to learn the language himself. Nothing seems impossible for this man, who now enthralls audiences from London to Los Angeles with his patchy but witty English.

Menstrual Man, a documentary on his life and work, was released in 2013. The film has been shown in several schools and film festivals across the world, and has been much appreciated. The funds generated from the film were utilized to fund generators for production for some of the self-help groups, because they get only a few hours of electricity daily.

Despite all the fame, Muruganantham has his eyes set on the distant goal of making India a country where all menstruating women use sanitary napkins; providing livelihood to one million rural women and even producing low-cost baby and adult diapers.

For the Innovator in You

"Do not try to do simple things in a complicated manner; rather, try to do complicated things in a simple manner.

Do not measure success by money or fame, but by the social impact of your work. Do something that helps others make money and you would definitely make good money for yourself in the process, without consciously trying to do so.

Do not be afraid of failure. Always remember that the difference between a stumbling block and a stepping stone is how high you raise your foot."

Deepak Ravindran – CEO, Innoz Technologies

Offline Internet on Mobile Phones

Using the internet means being online, right?

Wrong!

Deepak and his team have achieved the oxymoronic offline internet – a way to remain connected to the internet without being connected to it.

It all started in 2005 when Deepak joined a bachelor's degree program in Computer Science and Engineering at Lal Bahadur Shastri College of Engineering in Kasaragod, Kerala. He soon became friends with Mohd. Hisamuddin, Ashwin Nath and Abhinav Sree.

The bunks and strikes in college allowed them enough time for their common passion – tinkering with technology. They started working as freelance web developers, work they found thrilling, and which also gave them independence and confidence. Together, the four backbenchers also had a lot of fun in college.

Deepak recalls, "One day, a beautiful girl passed by us in college. One of my friends remarked that he would like to know how to impress a girl like her. Another friend replied, 'Run a Google Search'.

However, he did not have a laptop at that time. The only device available was a simple mobile phone, not even a smartphone."

That was early 2008; smartphones and mobile internet were yet to make their mark in India.

"It struck us that many people might need important information on the go or at places where there was limited or no internet coverage. We thought a system that would enable access to information anywhere, anytime, with just a basic phone, without logging on to the internet, would be extremely useful."

Thus were born the Google guys of the mobile world.

"We started researching on how web search algorithms work, that is, how they interpret the query and extract relevant data.

We envisioned a system where the user could send a query by SMS and the system would send an SMS in response, with the answer.

The challenge was that unlike normal Web search, we could not send URLs of relevant websites to the user, as he would be unable to access them without an internet connection. So, we had to devise a completely unique algorithm to compile the answer to the query in a meaningful text reply. This required intelligent and accurate interpretation of both the query and the search results.

It took us several months to develop the algorithm, but by mid-2008, we were ready with a fully functional system. We started telling our friends about it. They told their friends in turn and word quickly spread to almost all engineering campuses in Kerala. The users liked it a lot and the number of queries started swelling. However, as the user base grew, we started running out of resources to support the activity.

At that time, we did not have any idea about how to scale up the service or make it financially viable. We were just students who had let their imagination run wild and were basking in the glory.

Somehow, a local newspaper heard about the service and published an article on it. This was noticed by the business incubator at Technopark, Thiruvananthapuram and they approached us for incubation.

At that time, we had no idea about a business plan or revenue model. Our ambitions were limited to getting a decent job. All of us came from a middle-class background and had no idea about running a company.

Technopark offered us an office space and the opportunity to connect with investors. However, we were not prepared and turned down the offer.

Luckily for us, the Technopark authorities refused to take no for an answer. They offered us the alternative of Virtual Incubation. We would get the office address and expertise, but were not required to be physically present there. The arrangement suited us, because we could continue to pursue our degree in college.

It was only then that we started thinking about it as a serious business. Innoz Technologies was incorporated in September 2008. By that time, we already had good traffic and needed money to keep the system running. So, we approached friends and family who would be willing to help us out. Whatever money we could manage, we put into perfecting the technology, based on user feedback.

While we were making good headway with product development, our attendance at college was falling short. We were just one semester short of graduating, but the college authorities started creating a big fuss about the attendance. They thought that if they were lenient with us, it would set a bad example for others and enforcing attendance rules would be tougher."

Around the same time, IIM Ahmedabad's Centre for Innovation, Incubation and Entrepreneurship (CIIE) started the technology business incubation program, called iAccelerator.

"We received an invitation from IIM-A to be part of iAccelerator's first batch in 2009. It was a great opportunity, but we had to spend the next few months at the IIM-A campus. This meant that we would need to skip the semester, which essentially meant dropping out of college.

When we told our parents about it, they were strictly against the idea. However, our minds were already made up. After having seen how Technopark could help us, we simply did not want to let go of this opportunity.

We lied to our parents that we would eventually be awarded a degree from IIM-A. They were not convinced, but they knew we would not budge from our decision. So, they had to give up.

We moved to IIM-A in March 2009. iAccelerator proved to be a well-planned, three-month grooming program for budding entrepreneurs. By the end of the program, we had a revenue model in mind and knew that we would need to tie up with cellular service providers in order to monetize the service.

Toward the end of the program, we secured our first angel investment from Freeman Murray, who runs a Bengaluru-based creative community called Jaaga (www.jaaga.in).

After IIM-A, we came back to Technopark and applied for a patent for the technology. Meanwhile, we started to brainstorm over the future course of action." Ultimately, it was decided that Deepak would move to Gurgaon, in order to pitch the service to the various telecom companies headquartered there. The others would continue working on the technological aspects of the product.

In Gurgaon, Deepak faced a kind of reverse age discrimination. "A 21-year-old CEO would not be surprising in Silicon Valley, but here in India, it was not something people were used to. Whichever company I went to, senior executives would look at me suspiciously when I told them that I was the CEO of a Kerala-based technology company. Sometimes, the promised meetings wouldn't materialize; at other times, I would be told that everything about the idea was too immature.

It seemed funny and frustrating at the same time that experienced executives failed to see the potential of the idea and were more concerned about my appearance."

After several rejections, just when everything seemed dark, good luck finally shone on Innoz.

"After a failed meeting at Airtel, I was sulking in the cafeteria within the Airtel campus. A gentleman came over for a cup of coffee and chose to sit right next to me. By chance, I glanced at the card hanging around his neck. It read, 'Head, New Products, Airtel'.

I knew I had to pitch to him before he was done with his coffee. I didn't even think for a minute. I quickly introduced myself and got into a monologue about the product and its market potential.

He seemed very impressed and promised to take the case forward at Airtel."

As they say, a lot can indeed happen over a cup of coffee.

"It did not take long after that to sign a deal with Airtel. The service, branded SMS Gyaan, went live with Airtel in late 2011.

The users could send any query via SMS to 55444. The query was received by our server and interpreted by the algorithm. Web crawlers then looked for the relevant information on the internet. Finally, the information collected was compiled into a meaningful answer less than 480 characters long and sent back to the user via SMS. The whole process took just a few milliseconds, that is, almost an instantaneous response, much like the search engines on the internet.

Users were charged ₹ 1 per SMS. They also had the option to enroll for a monthly subscription of ₹ 30 which allowed them unlimited queries. Around 30% of this revenue was passed on to us."

In 2011, Innoz was listed among the Top 100 Global Companies by *Red Herring* magazine. This is a highly respected award among technology companies across the world and is a mark of technical excellence. The awardees are decided based on several criteria, such as sophistication of technology, social impact, disruptiveness, growth rate and market size.

"I had to go to the US to attend the award ceremony but had no money, because Airtel had yet to make the payments," Deepak remembers. "So, I started cold-calling and emailing some of the big names in the Indian IT industry for help. After reaching out to several people, I turned to Infosys CEO Kris Gopalakrishnan, who also hails from Kerala.

Not only did he reply, but also assured his full support. He was so impressed by our work that he wanted to be a part of the company as an investor. That's how we got our second angel investment. Soon, other angel investors followed and funding crossed the ₹ 1-crore mark."

The same year, NASSCOM named Innoz among Emerge: League of 10, a list of the 10 most promising technology start-ups in the country.

"With the kind of response the service received from Airtel subscribers, other telecom operators also jumped on the bandwagon. This time, they were chasing us, rather than the other way around.

Then, venture capitalist Mahesh Murthy's Seed Fund Advisors invested $3 million and our valuation shot through the roof.

By the end of 2012, we opened offices in Delhi, Mumbai and Bengaluru. The annual revenue stood at ₹ 6 crore, with a healthy profit margin. We generated ₹ 25-30 crore of additional revenue for the telecom companies that worked with us.

There was no looking back after that. In 2012-13, the revenue more than doubled, reaching ₹ 13 crore. In 2013-14, it crossed ₹ 20 crore."

Started by four people in their hostel room, Innoz is now a team of 60 people. The service is available with all telecom operators in the country and has 180 million active users. So far, SMS Gyaan has serviced 1.3 billion queries and receives almost 35 million queries a month. That is a daily average of over 1 million queries. Innoz has partnered with Wikipedia, Bing, Wolfram Alpha, Facebook, Twitter, SnapDeal, JustEat, DreamCricket, Carwaale, Zomato, Rotten Tomatoes and several databases that aggregate data on health, transport, sports, music and so on to offer value-added services based on their content and platform. For example, you can now SMS #CRI to 55444 to receive the latest cricket scores, SMS #FB <Your Message> to post to your Facebook status or use #TWEETS <Your Message> to post to Twitter. You can use the services in English or in Hindi (typed using the English alphabet). In fact, you can use #TRANS to convert text from any language to any language. You can even send an email, play word games, check PNR status of a train booking, or get weather information or the lyrics of a song.

"We started with the idea of being a mobile-based SMS answer engine, but we are now into all mobile-based web services. Over 10,000 hash tags are available for interacting with the web via SMS."

Innoz has recently partnered with the Swedish global phone directory service TrueCaller to allow users to look up for information related to a mobile number via SMS. Users can send an SMS to 55444 in the following format: TRACE <10 digit mobile number>, following which they will receive an SMS with information like the person's name, their service provider, region and service type (GSM or CDMA).

"We have turned every phone into a smartphone and transformed the good old SMS into its new avatar, SMS 2.0."

In a country of more than a billion people, only about 200 million people have access to a reliable internet connection. On the other hand, there are almost 560 million mobile phone users, of which only about 60 million use smartphones. Thus, this technology has great potential to serve the underserved.

"Almost 60% of our users come from Tier 2 and Tier 3 cities. More importantly, our users consist of all age groups, which means that many in the older generation, who may not be comfortable using the internet on a computer, can now access internet using a simple SMS."

Furthermore, for those who are yet to gain access to a reliable internet connection, Innoz provides the only way of connecting to the information expressway.

"Recently, we have started to expand abroad. With this international focus, we have rebranded SMS Gyaan as SmartSMS. We now have a foothold in many African and South Asian countries. We are even looking at the developed countries in North America and the Middle East, where mobile internet is already present in a big way.

Despite the availability of mobile internet in the developed world, the service can still be very useful, because mobile internet can sometimes fail to function for a variety of reasons.

We are now capable of running searches for pictures and videos. The next challenge for us is developing a system that can push ads according to user behavior."

Innoz is also in talks with handset manufacturers for an inbuilt SMS Gyaan application. This will reduce the service's dependence on mobile service providers and enable more people to use it. Deepak adds that they have also opened their platform to third-party app developers.

Though the Innoz founders have achieved tremendous success, they have not forgotten their roots. In 2012, they worked with the Kerala government to set up Startup Village, a technology business incubator at Kochi.

Startup Village aims to launch 1,000 technology start-ups over the next 10 years and hopes to host the next billion-dollar Indian company. It is focused on student start-ups and innovation in information and communication technologies. It is India's first incubator started with public–private partnership; many telecom and IT companies, in addition to Innoz, have contributed to it.

Deepak serves on the board of Startup Village, and under his aegis, the incubator has pioneered a movement in college campuses in Kerala called "30 Days to Freedom". This movement aims to convince college authorities to grant 20% relaxation in attendance to student entrepreneurs. So, unlike the Innoz founders, other technological geniuses will hopefully not need to drop out of their degree programs to pursue their dreams.

In order to make up for the lack of quality education in engineering institutions, Startup Village launched a program called Developer 1000 in early 2013 with an aim to churn out 1,000 app developers by the end of the year. The response has been tremendous. So far, about 3,500 programmers have been trained toward excellence in app development. Startup Village has also helped these programmers release more than 200 apps. The incubator also organizes all-expenses-paid trips to Silicon Valley for promising start-ups, so that they can experience the famed innovation and entrepreneurship culture of the Valley.

Innoz is now the biggest recruiter for the college from where its founders could not graduate. Moreover, the professors who once gave them an earful cannot stop praising them.

But this is not the end of their journey; it is just the beginning.

According to a UN survey, only 2.8 billion of the world's 7 billion people have access to any internet-enabled device. However, 6 billion people have access to mobile phones, of which 5 billion use a simple phone (that is, one that does not support internet connectivity). Thus, by connecting the unconnected, these youngsters have a big opportunity to change the world for good.

For the Innovator in You

"On millions of occasions, people will mock you or simply suggest that quitting would be a better option. In the end, it is your dream, your passion, and thus, your responsibility to not give up and convert your ideas into reality.

Never keep your product in stealth mode for long. Get it out into the hands of your potential users as soon as possible, collect feedback and work on improving the product.

As far as raising funds is concerned, consider yourself a storyteller. You need to have a convincing story and then you need to reach as wide an audience as possible, before you start getting the applause."

IdeaForge Team: (L to R) Ankit Mehta, Vipul Joshi, Ashish Bhat,
Amardeep Singh and Rahul Singh

Netra UAV

Do you remember the scene from the film *3 Idiots* where Rancho (Aamir Khan) flies a camera-fitted "helicopter" into the room of his college-mate (the character named Joy Lobo, played by Ali Fazal, who started with that project in the first place but ran into difficulties with the eccentric Principal), only to find him hanging from the ceiling?

Back from reel to real life, meet the real-life Ranchos; not three, but five idiots – Ankit Mehta, Ashish Bhat, Rahul Singh, Amardeep Singh and Vipul Joshi.

Ankit, Ashish, Rahul and Amardeep completed their engineering education at IIT Bombay and formed a very close bond. However, unlike the protagonists of the movie, they, thankfully, did not get into any trouble with the college administration.

Ankit completed a five-year BTech/MTech dual degree in Mechanical Engineering, specializing in Computer Aided Designing (CAD). He graduated in 2005 and eventually started IdeaForge in 2006 along with Rahul and Ashish, Ankit's junior in college. Rahul had a Mechanical Engineering degree, while Ashish had graduated in Electrical Engineering. Amardeep joined the company full-time, once he graduated with a dual degree in Aerospace Engineering in 2008. Vipul Joshi, who is Ankit's childhood friend, has an MBA degree from Switzerland and is a technology enthusiast. He joined the team to support them on the non-technical side of the business.

While the rest of the team was toiling hard to complete a very big order, I spoke to Ankit in detail about the story behind Netra.

Ankit was born in Pali, a small town near Jodhpur in Rajasthan. He was a very inquisitive and creative child, often wondering how a bridge was built or why a dam was needed to produce electricity. On their frequent evening walks, Ankit's father would narrate stories of great men who had achieved a lot despite lack of resources and adverse circumstances. That motivated Ankit to be an achiever, so that some father, some day, would narrate his story to their offspring.

During his class X, he learned about the IITs and the difficulties of getting admission. Instantly, he decided to tame the JEE beast.

With this aim, he went to Kota after class X to prepare for IIT-JEE. During those years, he immersed himself so much in the sciences that he was ranked among the top 100 at the Chemistry and Physics Olympiads in the country. A selection into IIT followed in the year 2000.

"IIT was nothing like I imagined. It provided a very liberal environment, where one could pursue whatever they wanted to. In my first year, I was actively involved with cricket, dance, dramatics and debating. In the second year, IIT-B's Mechanical Engineering department launched a robotics competition called Yantriki. The participants were required to make a water-playing robot which would compete in a real pool. That was my first endeavor in putting technology to use. It interested me so much that I started focusing all my energies on it.

I took tutelage under Dr Amarnath, a renowned IIT-B professor in the field of robotics. I used to come up with ideas and then bug him for financial support and guidance."

Some faculty members initiated an Innovation Cell at IIT-B with the aim to promote the growth of innovation on campus and help innovators with the patenting process and other requirements. Unfortunately, the response from students was low. In late 2001, with Dr Amarnath's support, Ankit started organizing seminars and workshops through the Innovation Cell, inviting eminent personalities from the field of science and technology. During this time, he got to know Ashish and Rahul really well and found out that they were equally passionate about robotics.

In 2003, the three of them together made a robot to participate in Robocon 2003.

Robocon, short for Robotic Contest, is an annual event organized by the Asia Pacific Broadcasting Union (ABU) with participation from over 50 countries. It is a two-stage event. In the first stage, teams from various technical universities in each country participate in a national competition. In the second stage, the winners from each country represent their country in the international competition.

Unfortunately, Ankit, Rahul and Ashish failed to win the national competition.

"It was a great learning experience for us. We decided to perfect our skills further and prepare better for next year's competition," Ankit says.

Their robot again failed them in 2004. However, they took it in their stride and vowed to come back stronger in the next edition.

In 2005, Ankit was in the final year. The final-year project, along with several other academic and non-academic responsibilities, left him little time to participate actively in the Robocon effort. Ashish and Rahul took it upon themselves and Ankit helped them whenever they required assistance.

Their persistence was rewarded this time. They won the competition in Pune and flew to Beijing to represent India at Robocon 2005.

"It was a mind-blowing experience. There were teams from MIT and several other top schools across the world. It was hard to imagine what they had already implemented with their robots. The design and build quality of their robots was way better than ours and we have no shame in admitting that we could not match them. What we learned there was to change our lives eventually. We came to understand that the quality of design and build were important for product performance; that is, a product is more than just the sum of its parts."

When Ankit graduated from IIT-B, he was awarded the Institute Technical Special Mention for his contributions in improving the technical scenario at the institute.

Ankit did not participate in the final-year placements; neither did he apply to any foreign university. His vision was to form a company and try to build innovative products.

"Once a friend asked me, '*Yaar tune* placement *bhi nahin li aur US university ka* backup plan *bhi nahin rakha.* Company *start karna chahta hai, tujhe bilkul darr nahi lagta?*' (You didn't appear for campus placements; nor do you have the backup plan of applying to a US university. You want to start a company; don't you ever feel scared about your future?)

The next day, I went for an early morning walk around the IIT campus. I was engrossed in thinking what success actually meant; whether it meant money, fame or adulation. And if it is any of these, did it matter if you got it at the age of 25 or 52?

I thought Mozart, by the time he died at the age of 35, immortalized his name in the world of music; but Jane Austen, on the other hand, could not get even a single work published till the age of 35. Does that make Jane Austen any less successful than Mozart? Of course not!

So, I decided I would not be part of any rat race. I would do what makes me happy, irrespective of how much and when the money flows in."

However, during his last months in college, he did realize that he would require a lot of money and a team of smart people to start a company.

"So far, funding for my projects had come from the institute or corporate sponsors and my friends at IIT had lent a helping hand. However, from now on, they would not be there for support.

So, I decided to take up a job and save for some time. Luckily, I found a job off-campus with ZS Associates, a leading consulting firm. The salary was comparable to the highest offers made on campus that year. I worked with them for the next six months, saving most of my salary.

At the end of six months, I knew I had saved enough to survive comfortably for another six months. So, I quit.

Initially, my parents were disturbed that I had quit a well-paying job, but they knew where my heart lay. So, they did not question my decision much and I went back to Mumbai.

I had done so much work in the technology space over the last five years in college and did not want that to be wasted. I knew no company or even PhD programs would let me work on my ideas. I would need to work on their ideas, whether I liked it or not. Thus, I had to start my own company."

During college, Ankit had worked on developing a novel mechanical energy storage and release device. This was a power spring, wound in such a way that the energy density of the spring configuration, and thus, its energy storage capacity, was increased significantly. Ankit had a patent for the device and decided to use it to fabricate a mechanical cellphone charger. He believed that there would be a great market for the product in rural India.

He incorporated IdeaForge in 2006 with the help of Society for Innovation and Entrepreneurship (SINE), the business incubator which provides support to technology-based entrepreneurs at IIT Bombay.

Meanwhile, Ashish and Rahul had also graduated with top honors. Ashish, who also holds the distinction of designing the fastest Micromouse (a robot that solves an unknown given maze) in India, was awarded a Roll of Honour for his technical competence by the Student Gymkhana at IIT Bombay. It was after eight years that somebody had won this honor at the institute.

Instead of joining a top MNC or flying to greener pastures, both Ashish and Rahul joined Ankit at IdeaForge.

Together, they worked on making the mechanical charger a reality. The charger was aesthetically designed, was light and small, and thus, easy to carry around. One minute of rotating the charger handle provided enough charge for 30 minutes of standby time.

They travelled far and wide, to the remotest regions of the country and adopted all methods to sell their product, but the response was less than encouraging.

Through their professors at IIT-B, they got a project, backed by the DRDO, for creating data-logging systems for unmanned aerial vehicles (UAVs). A data-logging system is a piece of hardware that records the flight parameters of an aerial system (such as height, roll angle, air speed and acceleration). This initiated them into aerial vehicles.

They started supplying avionics (electronic systems used in airborne vehicles), and in due course of time, began work on developing their own UAV in association with a DRDO lab.

Rahul already had a great passion for hovercrafts and his experience with flying devices came in handy. Meanwhile, Amardeep graduated with a degree in Aerospace Engineering and joined them full-time, bringing in more expertise in that department. Vipul, who had worked for over a year with ArvinMeritor in Zurich as a Marketing Product Manager, also joined them.

In 2008, they exhibited the first indigenously built UAV at an exposition hosted by the Indian Army and the US Department of Defense.

Being first-timers did not stop them from being adjudged the best entry in the hover category (that is, vertical landing and takeoff category), despite tough competition from 16 products developed at some of the most respected technology universities and companies across the world.

"Not only were we the first to accomplish this in India, our UAV was controlled by the world's smallest and lightest auto-pilot (the microprocessor that enables controlling the UAV remotely), which was completely designed and fabricated by us. The UAV segment has very few players across the world and the applications so far have been restricted to military purposes.

Unlike most companies in the UAV space, which procure parts from outside vendors, we are completely vertically integrated. We make all the hardware and software ourselves, including the auto-pilot, air-train, ground communication and control software and the image processing software."

DRDO helped IdeaForge in several ways, such as in fine-tuning the efficacy and handling of the UAV in the field; understanding the needs of the targeted end-user, so that they could create a more user-friendly product; procuring the required material at a reduced cost through a rate contract; getting the product exhibited in the key defense related exhibitions, thus helping with the sales and so on. DRDO also signed a Technology Transfer memorandum of understanding (MoU) with IdeaForge. The product is often labeled as the DRDO Netra, in recognition of the support received from DRDO. "Association with DRDO also helps in generating positive recognition more easily," Ankit adds.

"In February 2010, we gave a demo of the UAV to the Defense Minister Shri AK Antony at the DefExpo in Delhi. The Indian Army was already looking to deploy UAVs for stealth operations along borders in difficult areas. The UAV was appreciated by all the concerned dignitaries. Ten prototypes were made and put through various tests, such as temperature (from -10°C to 55°C) and high-altitude tests. After successful trials, the UAV was cleared for production and induction.

Around the same time, *Mumbai Mirror*, a popular local newspaper in Mumbai, did a story on Netra. The actress Dia Mirza came across that article and suggested it to Rajkumar Hirani, the director, writer and editor of *Munnabhai* fame, who was working on *3 Idiots* at that time. Rajkumar Hirani contacted us and asked if he could use the UAV in one of the scenes.

3 Idiots gave us a lot of visibility and made it easy for us to explain to people about our product. However, the movie also set several other people in India on the path of experimenting with making the UAV.

After *3 Idiots*, several big orders flowed in, largely from the defense forces in India for use in anti-terror, counter-insurgency and border management operations.

From the very beginning, our focus was on quality and we matched the international standards, if not bettered them. We won tenders against tough competition from top international companies such as the Israeli company, Blue Bird Auro and the German company, Microdrone.

A lot of media coverage followed. We were first featured on CNBC Young Turks in 2008. In 2010, *India Today* placed us among the Top 20 Innovators Changing Lives. We were on Times Now Amazing Indians in 2011. The CNN-IBN

Young Leader Award was conferred on us in 2012. CNBC Young Turks covered us again in 2013."

In 2012, the Maharashtra Navnirman Sena (MNS) organized a rally at Azad Maidan in Mumbai to protest against the riots in Assam. A huge crowd was to gather and the Mumbai Police was under severe pressure to ensure that no untoward incident took place. They decided to deploy Netra for surveillance, making India the first country to use a UAV for crowd management.

Since then, the Ahmedabad city administration has shown great enthusiasm for obtaining Netra for crowd and traffic management, and it may soon become the first city in the world to do so.

In June 2013, after the devastating floods and landslides in Uttarakhand, the National Disaster Response Force (NDRF) called in Netra UAVs to help with the rescue operations.

"We responded by deploying four Netra UAVs within 24 hours. Despite the rough terrain and harsh weather, Netra did a superb job by locating 190 trapped survivors. It was a very difficult mission. It was a great responsibility and we are extremely proud that our baby – Netra – could help save so many valuable lives. This also opened the door for Netra to be used for another purpose – disaster management. We are now conducting training at our facility in Mumbai for organizations associated with disaster management."

Netra is fabricated from carbon fiber composites and weighs just 1.5 kg. It is equipped with a high-resolution daylight camera as well as a thermal camera for night vision. The cameras have a 10X optical zoom with pan and tilt control. The in-flight video can be transmitted live or be recorded on-board for analysis later. The best part of Netra is its image processing software that allows locking a particular image, which can then be used to track a particular target. Inbuilt image stabilization and defogging capabilities enable the device to operate in turbulent winds and hazy conditions. The device can monitor ground action up to a distance of 5 kilometers and zoom to focus on the minutest of details.

"The UAV is practically failsafe. If it is running low on battery or loses communication with the base station, it has the capability to return to the base station on its own. It is invisible to most of the commonly used radars and is practically noiseless.

Unlike the conventional helicopter which has only one rotor, Netra UAV employs quad-rotors, that is, four smaller rotors instead of one bigger rotor. This gives more stability to the UAV during flight. It also improves control and ensures that the UAV is able to fly even if a particular rotor fails for some reason.

The user interface is very simple and intuitive. Anybody can be trained to use Netra in just a few sessions. The position of the UAV is tracked and displayed on a map on the screen in real time and flight plan adjustment can be as simple as 'point and click'. Also, the user is automatically prompted for all the checklists, before and during the flight, to ensure that nothing is amiss.

Each Netra UAV costs several tens of lakhs, but is still much cheaper and more functional than several other UAVs available in the international market."

Ankit shares the company's future plans. "After establishing ourselves in India, we are looking at international expansion and have already identified distributors in New Zealand and Australia. Distributors in other geographical territories are also being approached. We are also working on enhancing the battery life, range and other capabilities of the UAV to make it even more attractive to potential buyers.

It has been an extremely difficult yet satisfying journey. Beginning with a small seed capital arranged from friends, family members and SINE, we have now crossed half-a-million dollars in sales and would be able to cross a million dollars in the current financial year. We expect to grow even faster in the coming years, as we expand our product portfolio and professional investors come onboard."

For the Innovator in You

"Never compromise on product quality and performance, even if it increases the cost. If the product is good, it will easily command a high price, and more importantly, it will bring in more discerning buyers. Cut corners and thou shall never pass.

Building a great team is important, as you will not be able to handle all aspects of product development yourself. Bring in people with complementary skills; give them clear responsibilities and the freedom to execute their ideas. Capable and dedicated people working in a motivational environment can do the unthinkable.

Do not be in a hurry in the product development phase. Take time to understand the needs of prospective buyers and the problems associated with the current set of solutions.

One final piece of advice is that do not count your chickens before they hatch. Anticipate hurdles, be prepared for them; and also accept the fact that despite the best preparations, there will still be situations that will leave you dumbstruck. In such circumstances... *dil pe haath rakh ke bolna, Chachu* All is Well, All is Well."

Epilogue

As can be observed from these stories, innovation and entrepreneurship are connected. Quoting the management guru Peter Drucker, "Innovation is the specific instrument of entrepreneurship. Innovation is the act that endows resources with a new capacity to create wealth."

As the inventor of a product, you are the best judge of its potential. There will be many naysayers who will not understand what your product is about, but the best way to prove them wrong is to sell it yourself. You may not have sold a toothpick before, but as they say – there is always a first time. You will learn the art like many others in this book did. You can learn from their mistakes, but do not be afraid to make your own.

The set of stories presented here give a good overview of the scope and scale of innovation occurring in Indian academic and industrial circles. However, for every person presented in the book, there are several others whose work still needs to be talked about. It would be my constant effort to bring out many more such stories.

I salute each and every one of those whose work has fetched and will continue to fetch glory to the country. Their vision will help change the perception of India as a country with insignificant technological output.

Appendix I
Patent and Prosper

By Mrinmayee Bhushan

The motivation to write this article comes from my very own experience with patents – the good, the bad and the ugly.

I am a first-generation entrepreneur and had little experience with product development and idea protection when I started. I learned it all by getting my fingers burned.

After spending loads of hard-earned money toward the fee of patent attorneys in India and the US, I ended up drafting, prosecuting and receiving the grant of four patents on my own. I also had to abandon a very valuable US patent after a very costly, long-drawn prosecution of a patent application that was badly botched up by the patent attorneys.

I hope my experiences will help fellow innovators fumble a little less while patenting their innovations.

What is a patent, and why bother getting one?

A patent is a form of intellectual property, which consists of a set of exclusive rights granted by a sovereign state to an inventor or their assignee for a limited period of time, in exchange for public disclosure of the invention. That is, a patent restricts others from making direct commercial use of the invention, but this restriction applies only for a limited period of time.

Patentability

The patentability of your innovation needs to be established at the earliest. Though patent laws and practices vary from one country to another, there are three main criteria on which an innovation is said to be patentable subject matter:

1. It is a novelty.
2. It is non-obvious.
3. It has industrial applicability/utility.

An innovator working in a bootstrapping model can do an initial patentability search himself by searching patent databases, such as the US Patent office (USPTO) database, consisting of patent applications and already granted patents. The European Patent Office database (espacenet), databases of relevant scientific publications and other electronic databases such as Google Scholar can be good resources as well.

This initial scrutiny helps the innovator in estimating the patentability of the subject matter before spending anything on a patent agent. This effort, in turn, results in minimal search charges by the attorney.

Patent Drafting

A provisional or complete specification should be filed before publishing any article or news item in the public domain.

Usually, the patent is drafted meticulously by a competent patent agent in consultation with the innovator. The layout of a patent application typically consists of Abstract, Prior art, Technical details/drawings, Examples, Summary and Claims.

If an innovator decides to draft and prosecute his patent application, then studying different types of patent applications in the relevant subject matter helps to understand the nuances of the patenting system. Studying the USPTO patent drafting rules is particularly useful, because these are stricter than rules in other patent offices.

Innovator's Dilemma

Drafting patent claims is an art. The language of the claims is of critical importance, because the set of claims defines the scope of protection sought by the patent application. However, though the patent application is examined on the basis of what is "claimed", the body of complete specification is extremely important. The complete specification should sufficiently describe the subject matter for a person skilled in the art (relevant field) to understand it. During the prosecution of the patent application, the applicant is allowed to edit/change/cancel or add new patent claims, only if it is supported by the complete specification. Any claim without the support of the specification is treated as "new subject matter" and is not allowed to be included.

This is the "not too much, not too little" dilemma for an innovator.

The Mother of the Invention

Every innovator must remember the fact that they are the mother of their invention. If it is truly novel, no one in this world understands the subject matter of your innovation as you do.

The innovator must be totally involved when the patent agent is drafting the patent application. You may not be conversant with legal language used in the patent application. However, do not simply send a write-up of the subject matter to the patent agent and expect him to draft a competitive patent specification and claims. It is highly advisable to arrange multiple meetings with the agent during the process. During the very first meeting, howsoever complicated a technology one is dealing with, the innovator should explain the subject matter to the patent agent in layman's language, without using too much scientific jargon. (You can practice this by explaining your technology to a school-going child.)

This may sound very ridiculous, but an esteemed patent agent and a good friend practicing in the USPTO has taught me this technique of initially oversimplifying the subject matter. This helps the patent agent first understand the "crux of the matter" and then its intricacies.

At the time of drafting the very first provisional specification, the innovator may not have plans or resources to take it to the global level. However, if the technology has global potential, the specifications (provisional or complete) should be drafted according to international standards.

It is advisable to apply internationally through the World Intellectual Property Organization's (WIPO) Patent Cooperation Treaty (PCT). PCT's international search for patentability and written opinion and the international patent examination report form the basis for applying for patents in various countries separately. It helps the innovator in estimating the patentability of the innovation, before spending funds on examination by patent offices of individual countries. The patenting process is very time-sensitive. The innovator needs to adhere to the timeframes very stringently. The websites of Indian Patent Office and the WIPO PCT Time Limit Calculator are resources to help innovators meet these deadlines.

Though patent agents are aware of the time limits of every stage of patenting, the innovator is strongly advised to be involved in the process by studying and understanding patent laws and rules. It is extremely important for those innovators who are working in a bootstrapping model.

If relevant to your innovations, do add other forms of intellectual property such as trademarks and copyrights to make your patent basket more valuable.

In a nutshell

If you are ready to take the extra effort of studying patent laws and want to prosecute your own patents, without hiring the services of professionals, here's how to go about it:

a. As mentioned earlier, study other patent applications and patent laws extensively.
b. Apply internationally through PCT as an individual, which results in reduction of various fees.
c. You do not need a patent agent to apply to PCT.
d. In addition, some countries like the US, the UK, Australia and Canada allow individual applicants to prosecute their own applications.
e. Reduce the risk by consulting a friendly patent agent as necessary, instead of authorizing him to act on your behalf.
f. After the patent is granted, do not assign it to your own company, until you license out or sell the technology. The annual patent fees are very low for an individual, so keep the patent assigned to an individual (innovator).

The Ministry for Small and Medium Enterprises (Government of India) provides patent reimbursement to SMEs to encourage patenting (₹ 25,000 for Indian patents and ₹ 200,000 for international patents). However, it can be more expensive for an innovator or his start-up company to maintain the patents, because the annual maintenance fees are much higher for companies, as compared to individuals.

Some useful links

http://www.ipindia.nic.in/
http://www.wipo.int/pct/en/calculator/pct-calculator.html
http://www.uspto.gov/
http://www.epo.org/searching/free/espacenet.html

Note: These suggestions are especially useful for individual innovators pursuing innovation with very limited resources. They may not necessarily be the best practices applicable to everybody and in all situations. In any case, it is definitely better for innovators to know the patenting process, even if they can afford the steep patenting fee.

About the Author

Akshat Agrawal is a Mechanical Engineer from IIT Delhi. During his IIT days, he was involved in a very innovative initiative – the design and fabrication of an artificial knee joint for above-the-knee amputees. Therefore, he has had first-hand experience of the difficulties that innovators face.

He is also an avid traveler and has traveled to 22 countries in three continents, living in the US and Europe for a considerable period of time. India remains his first love, however, and he currently resides here with his family.

Akshat is currently a Director at Alpha Beta Classes, an innovative start-up in online and offline education that aims to improve access to quality education for millions of children in India.

Akshat is also passionate about writing and is an award-winning short-story writer.

He can be reached at istory@gmail.com

JAICO PUBLISHING HOUSE

Elevate Your Life. Transform Your World.

ESTABLISHED IN 1946, Jaico Publishing House is home to world-transforming authors such as Sri Sri Paramahansa Yogananda, Osho, The Dalai Lama, Sri Sri Ravi Shankar, Sadhguru, Robin Sharma, Deepak Chopra, Jack Canfield, Eknath Easwaran, Devdutt Pattanaik, Khushwant Singh, John Maxwell, Brian Tracy and Stephen Hawking.

Our late founder Mr Jaman Shah first established Jaico as a book distribution company. Sensing that independence was around the corner, he aptly named his company Jaico ('Jai' means victory in Hindi). In order to service the significant demand for affordable books in a developing nation, Mr. Shah initiated Jaico's own publications. Jaico was India's first publisher of paperback books in the English language.

While self-help, religion and philosophy, mind/body/spirit, and business titles form the cornerstone of our non-fiction list, we publish an exciting range of travel, current affairs, biography, and popular science books as well. Our renewed focus on popular fiction is evident in our new titles by a host of fresh young talent from India and abroad. Jaico's recently established Translations Division translates selected English content into nine regional languages.

In addition to being a publisher and distributor of its own titles, Jaico is a major national distributor of books of leading international and Indian publishers. With its headquarters in Mumbai, Jaico has branches and sales offices in Ahmedabad, Bangalore, Bhopal, Chennai, Delhi, Hyderabad, Kolkata and Lucknow.

SINCE 1946